Practical
Diving

TOM MOUNT and
AKIRA J. IKEHARA

Practical

Diving

A Complete Manual for Compressed Air Divers

UNIVERSITY OF MIAMI PRESS
Coral Gables, Florida

Designed by Bernard Lipsky

Manufactured in the United States of America

Library of Congress Cataloging in Publication Data

Mount, Tom.
   Practical diving.

   Bibliography: p.
   Includes index.
   1. Skin diving. 2. Diving, Submarine.
I. Ikehara, Akira J., 1940-   joint author.
II. Title.
GV840.S78M64 1975   797.2'3 75-1059
ISBN 0-87024-278-4

Contents

Illustrations

Tables

Foreword

Practical Diving was developed to meet a need of the University of Miami research diving program. It also meets a need of the general diving community. Advanced training for sport divers is currently being emphasized by the major national certification agencies. The National YMCA SCUBA Program has recommended this text as a primary reference for its Advanced Diver training program.

This recommendation is well founded. The authors of *Practical Diving* have done an excellent job of compiling the latest state-of-the-art in diving technology and presenting it in a well-organized manner, conducive to assimilation by an audience with a wide range of diving interests and capabilities. This publication contains information unavailable in any other general diving manual. The validity of this information is assured by the professional credibility of its authors. *Practical Diving* represents a major contribution to the diving industry.

ROBERT W. SMITH
Chairman, National YMCA SCUBA Committee

Preface

Upon descending into the sea, we discover the intriguing world of inner-space. In this world we can discover much about ourselves, our origin and continuation. By observing the behavior of underwater animals we can learn much about our own behavior. In this world of beauty, color, fish, and corals, a mood overcomes us and suspends us from our normal lives, teaching and relaxing us simultaneously.

Diving has become widespread as a tool for research, as a commercial vehicle, and as a means of sport and relaxation for thousands of divers. With over 100,000 divers being trained annually, the popularity of diving obviously is increasing.

This text has been written to fill the need for a book that will enable the diver to develop a complete understanding of both the practical and the theoretical aspects of diving and diving physiology. It is our opinion as authors that with a thorough knowledge and careful application of the theory and practical skills discussed herein, diving can and will be safe.

TOM MOUNT

Acknowledgments

I wish to extend my thanks to the following for their assistance, recommendations, and support in writing this book: the University of Miami Rosenstiel School of Marine and Atmospheric Science, Mr. Jim Gibbons, Dr. Don de Sylva, Dr. Jon Staiger, Mr. Bruce Chalker, Dr. William H. Hulet, Mr. Dave Desautels, Mr. Robert Smith, Dr. Glen Egstrom, Ms. Sue Lucksted, and Rick Freshee.

Practical
Diving

1

Physical Aspects of the Diving Environment

Before discussing man in the water, special consideration must be given to the environment he is about to enter. Survival depends on physiological adaption of man, and this adaption depends on an understanding of physics. By definition, physics is the study of the properties of matter and how matter behaves under varying conditions.

Matter is anything that occupies space and has weight. It exists in three states: liquid (incompressible, having a definite volume and conforming to the shape of its container); gas (compressible, having no definite volume or shape); and solid (incompressible, having a definite volume and shape).

Gases and mixtures of gases are of major importance to man and life. Normally man breathes a gas mixture called air, which is composed of 20.94% oxygen (O_2, colorless, tasteless, odorless, capable of supporting life, and combustible; in high concentrations it is a cellular toxin) and 79% nitrogen (N_2, colorless, odorless, tasteless, inert, incapable of supporting life, and intoxicating at high pressure). Carbon dioxide (CO_2), which constitutes .04% of air, is another gas of major importance; it is the by-product of burning organic material and of the normal oxidation of food in the body. In high concentrations CO_2 has harmful effects on the diver.

Understanding problems encountered by the diver in the water requires an understanding of pressure, buoyancy, temperature, and the conduction of sound and light waves.

Pressure

Pressure is the amount of force per unit area. Pressure is measured in pounds per square inch (psi), dynes, atmospheres (atm.), or millimeters (mm) of mercury (Hg). These measurements express the force the gas or liquid exerts in all directions.

If a column of air reached from sea level to the upper limits of the atmosphere, we would say it exerted a pressure of one atmosphere or that the weight of the earth's atmosphere at sea level is equal to one atmosphere (1 atm.) or 14.7 pounds per square inch of pressure. For better understanding, atmospheric pressure can be further broken down into these units:

1 atm. = 760 mm Hg or 14.7 psi or 29.9 inches of mercury

If the column were filled with water instead of air, 33 feet of salt water would yield 760 mm Hg or 14.7 psi or a pressure equivalent to 1 atm. If freshwater were substituted for salt water, the column would have to extend 34 feet to yield a pressure of 1 atm. Thus for each 33 feet of descent in salt water 1 atm. of pressure is gained; due to a difference in density, in freshwater 1 atm. is gained every 34 feet.

Table 1. Pressure and Altitude or Depth Relations

Altitude and depth (in feet)	Pressure (in atm.)	Psi
30,000	.30	4.41
18,000	.50	7.35
10,000	.69	10.14
5,000	.83	12.20
Sea level	1.00	14.70
33	2.00	29.40
99	4.00	58.80
297	10.00	147.00
1,000	31.30	460.10

NOTE: In freshwater 1 atm. of pressure is gained every 34 feet; thus, if the depths listed were for freshwater they would be 34, 102, 306, and 1,030.

For convenience the term psig (pounds per square inch gauge) is frequently used. The difference between psi and psig is that psi refers to the total or true pressure, whereas psig is the difference between atmospheric pressure and the pressure being measured. For example,

1 atm. = 14.7 psi or 0 psig and 2 atm. = 29.4 psi or 14.7 psig

Most gauges used by divers (depth gauges, tank pressure gauges) are calibrated in psig's.

Liquid Pressure

The pressure produced by a liquid is a direct result of its weight, which in turn is the effect of gravity on the molecules of the liquid. When comparing weights of objects we use the term density. Salt water has a density of 64 pounds per cubic foot. Freshwater has a density of 62.4 pounds per cubic foot. Since water is, for all practical purposes, incompressible, its density remains constant regardless of depth. As a result the pressure of water is proportional to the depth. For example, if a tank is filled to 99 feet with salt water, the pressure will be 99 times 64 or 6,336 pounds per square foot on the bottom. To convert this to psig, divide by 144 (12 inches per foot squared). The result, 44.1 psig, can then be converted to psi by adding 1 atm. of pressure from sea level [44.1 (psig, water pressure) + 14.7 (psig the pressure at sea level) = 58.1 psi].

For convenience it is easier to determine pressure increase per foot in salt water by multiplying the depth in feet by .445 (for freshwater this number is .432). This water pressure or psig can then be converted to psi by adding 14.7.

When we are aware of the high pressures exerted at depth, it is only natural to wonder how these pressures will affect our bodies. We must first consider that man is approximately 98% liquids and solids and 2% air spaces. The laws governing fluids are:

If pressure is applied to the surface of a fluid, the pressure is transmitted to all parts of that fluid.

The pressure at any point in a fluid is the same in all directions if the fluid is at rest.

In a homogeneous liquid the pressure at all points on the horizontal plane is equal.

Pascal's Principle: In a liquid in a confined space, pressure is transmitted equally in all directions. Thus, even though a man is exposed to approximately 82,000 pounds of pressure at 33 feet underwater, this pressure is transmitted throughout his body shell and he is not crushed (see Figure 1).

Only those areas of the body containing air spaces offer potential problem areas. These air spaces can be equalized, however, through one of several methods (see chapter 3).

Gas Laws

Most physiological reactions of man, such as barotrauma (pressure injury), pulmonary barotrauma, decompression sickness, inert gas narcosis,

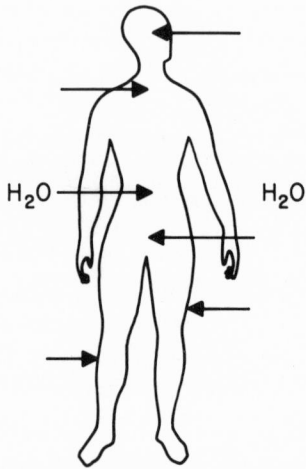

Fig. 1. Diagram showing the equal distribution
of pressure throughout the body.

oxygen poisoning, carbon dioxide poisoning, and decreased respiratory efficiency, are governed by the gas laws.

Perhaps one of the most important gas laws, and definitely the first one a diver becomes aware of, is Boyle's Law.

Boyle's Law

The pressure (P) of a given gas varies inversely as its volume (V) at a constant temperature. Mathematically Boyle's Law can be stated as

$$PV = k \text{ or } P_1 V_1 = P_2 V_2$$

It can be seen that an increase in pressure is followed by a corresponding decrease in volume (see Table 2).

Table 2. Pressure and Volume Relations

Depth, feet	Atm.	Air volume, %	Sphere radius,%
sea level	1	V = 100	R = 100
33	2	V = 50	R = 79.5
66	3	V = 33.3	R = 69.3
99	4	V = 25	R = 63

Table 2 shows that compression of the air spaces takes place during descent and expansion of these air spaces occurs during ascent. In a tank the greater density caused by depth results in more gas molecules being used to supply the diver's needs, thus reducing the time a given air supply will last. Also, greater density increases breathing resistance, resulting in decreased respiratory efficiency.

We can see that the percentage of change is less the deeper the diver goes. Thus the greater the depth, the less noticeable the pressure change. In a sphere, volume can be determined by

$$V = (4/3\pi)r^3$$

The term $4/3\pi$ is constant; thus, sphere radius (r) is a function of the cube root of volume. Due to volume being directly affected by pressure, radius is affected by the cube root of pressure. If we substitute $(4/3\pi)r^3$ for V in Boyle's Law, we get the following:

$$r^2 = 3r\sqrt[3]{P_1/P_2}$$

A balloon with a volume of 10 would have a radius of 1.34 feet; when the volume is reduced to 2.5 the radius is .843. This example shows that even though the volume was decreased to one-fourth its original volume, the radius remained over one-half its initial value. This fact becomes important when treating air embolism or decompression sickness. In both these maladies the radius is of greater importance than the volume of a bubble. From Table 2 and Figure 2 we can see that at a certain point additional changes in pressure have little effect on radius.

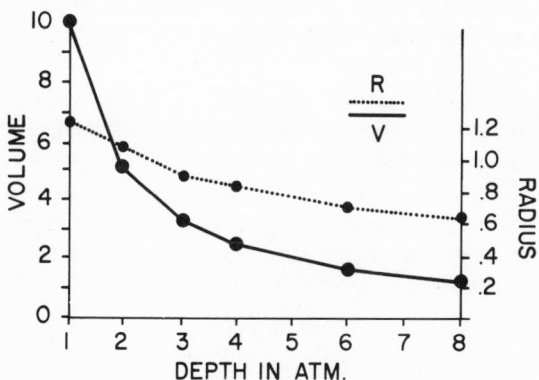

Fig. 2. Depth and subsequent changes in pressure, after a certain point, have little effect on radius.

Another important consideration of bubble size is surface area. Surface area of a sphere is equal to $r^2 4\pi$. Changes in radius have a greater effect on volume than on surface area. A pressure that causes a bubble radius change will cause a greater reduction in bubble volume than in surface area. This concept is important in treating decompression sickness, since the patient can be recompressed to a pressure which sufficiently reduces the bubble radius to permit blood to flow, but which retains a surface area large enough to effectively allow gas to diffuse from the bubble.

Charles' Law

If pressure is constant the volume is proportional to the temperature. This law simplifies the fact that temperature increases are followed by a corresponding increase in volume. A flexible container will expand therefore when left near heat. A rigid container such as a scuba bottle will reflect the increased volume by showing a higher pressure reading. We can see from this law that a warm scuba tank will appear to have a higher volume, as indicated by pressure, than a cool one, and thus tanks should be stored in cool places and charged slowly.

General Gas Law

This law combines Boyle's and Charles' laws and is expressed as

$$(P_1 V_1)/T_1 = (P_2 V_2)/T_2$$

where T is temperature.

Before further discussion of the general gas law let us briefly review the kinetic theory of gases. Every gas is a collection of molecules that are in continuous (kinetic) motion. If temperature is reduced, the motion is slowed. A temperature that would cease all molecular motion would be absolute zero. The theoretical value of absolute zero is $0°$ Kelvin ($-273.18°C$) or $0°$ Rankin ($-459.7°F$).

The more molecules that collide, the higher the pressure; or, the same number of molecules colliding in a smaller space will increase the pressure. This theory is again important in understanding pressure effects, density, and the need for establishing a zero temperature reference point.

For solving equations dealing with physics all values must be absolute; thus psig's must be changed to psi's. The general gas law is used to solve the following problems.

1. A diver uses 2 cubic feet of air per minute and is diving to 132 feet. What volume of gas must a compressor supply to meet his requirements?

   $P_1 = 5$ atm.
   $V_1 = 2$ cubic feet
   $T_1 = T_2$

P_2 = 1 atm. (sea level)

V_2 = ?

$V_2 = P_1V_1/P_2 = 5 \times 2/1 = 10$ cubic feet

2. A tank is charged to a pressure of 2,985.3 psig at a temperature of 140°F. What will the tank pressure be when the tank has cooled to 20°C? Note: Since the given temperatures are based on different scales, both temperatures must be converted to a common scale.

P_1 = 2,985.3 psig + 14.7 = 3,000 psi

$V_1 = V_2$

T_1 = 140°F + 460 = 600°R

P_2 = ?

T_2 = 20°C or 68°F + 460 = 528°R

where F = (C × 1.8) + 32.

P_2 = 2,640 psi or 2,625.3 psig

Temperatures can be converted to Kelvin instead of Rankin. The values then would be

T_1 = 140°F or 60°C + 273 = 333°K

where C = (F − 32)/1.8 and

T_2 = 20°C + 273 = 293°K

The final answer for P_2 would be the same.

Partial pressures are important to the diver's understanding of his body's functioning at the surface and also when exposed to increased pressures. Partial pressures are the parts of the total pressure exerted by each gas in the mixture of gases. For example, in air, oxygen represents 21% of the total mixture; thus, at sea level its partial pressure is 3.087 psi or 160 mm Hg. Nitrogen represents 79% of the mixture, or a partial pressure of 11.613 psi or 600 mm Hg. The law that describes partial pressures is Dalton's Law. Dalton's Law states that the total pressure exerted by a mixture of gases is the sum of the pressures that would be exerted by each gas if it alone were present and occupied the total volume.

From the preceding definition we can see that as total pressure increases, the partial pressures of each gas will also increase. To determine partial pressures at each depth the following steps must be taken:

1. Determine psig. (Saltwater psig is determined by multiplying depth

by .445. Freshwater psig is determined by multiplying depth by .432.)

2. Determine psi expressed as total pressure (P_T).
$P_T = psig + 14.7$

3. Determine individual partial pressure (P_P) of the gas in question.
$P_P = \%$ gas mixture of P_T

For example, oxygen is 21% of P_T and nitrogen is 79% of P_T.

The above values can be expressed in mm Hg or atm. pressures.

Partial pressures explain the effects that gases have as a result of changing environmental pressure. If the partial pressure of oxygen is dropped below 1.5 psi it will not sustain life; on the other hand, if it increases very much above 11 psi it can begin to have toxic effects on the body. Changes in the partial pressures of other gases also have severe effects on man.

Gas diffusion is the spreading or scattering of gas molecules. When two gases are brought together, they intermingle until they produce a uniform mixture. Molecular movement is random; however, gas will tend to mix from a greater pressure to a lower pressure. Therefore, if a higher partial pressure exists on one side of a membrane than another, the gas will tend to move toward the side with the lower partial pressure. Oxygen, for example, moves from the blood into tissue fluid around the cell and into the cell as a result of diffusion. The amount of oxygen in blood is greater than the amount in the cell, so the oxygen moves toward the area of lesser concentration. If the pressure (number of molecules) is equal on both sides, there will be no further shift of the gas. In oxygen diffusion a static equilibrium is never reached because the metabolic process continues to use oxygen. A dynamic equilibrium, however, is kept constant.

Solubility is the number of gas molecules a specific liquid will take up in solution at a given partial pressure and temperature. When equilibrium has been reached, the liquid contains an amount of dissolved gas proportional to the partial pressure of that gas in the mixture to which the liquid is exposed. Different gases have varying degrees of solubility for given liquids, for example, fat and water solubility are quite different. Fat will take up five times more dissolved nitrogen (N_2) than water. Other factors affecting solubility are temperature and pressure.

If two gases are present in the lungs at the same pressure, the quantity of gas that will go into solution depends on the solubility of the gas. Thus more of one gas will be dissolved than the other.

Henry's Law

The amount of gas at a constant temperature that will dissolve in a liquid is almost directly proportional to the partial pressure of that gas. The expression "almost" is the time factor. Gases do not reach a state of equilibrium instantly. For example, when a diver initially reaches a given depth, the gas uptake is rapid due to high pressure differential, but, as the state of equilibrium is being reached, the rate of saturation slows. Thus a tissue may become 90% saturated within 4 hours but will take up to 12 hours or longer before reaching total equilibrium. An understanding of gas solubility and uptake in the body is mandatory to understanding the development of decompression sickness.

Archimedes' Principle

Any object partially or wholly immersed in a liquid is buoyed up by a force equal to the weight of the liquid displaced.

A body will sink if the weight of the fluid it displaces is less than the weight of the body (negative buoyancy).
A body will neither sink nor float if the fluid it displaces is equal to its own weight (neutral buoyancy).
A body will float if the weight of the fluid it displaces is greater than the weight of the body (positive buoyancy).

To determine the theoretical buoyant force of a diver, we must determine how many cubic feet he displaces and the density of the water, and then we must determine the difference. For example, if a diver weighs 172 pounds and displaces 2.75 cubic feet of water, will he sink or float in salt water? In freshwater?

2.75 × 64 (density per cubic foot) = 176 pounds buoyant force

Since the diver's weight is four pounds lighter than the buoyant force of the water, the diver will float. In freshwater, this become

2.75 × 62.4 = 171.6 pounds buoyant force

so the diver will be negative buoyed by .4 pound.

Body characteristics have much to do with the buoyancy of the diver. Fat people tend to float better than lean or muscular people. As a rule women usually float better than men. Another factor affecting buoyancy is lung volume. In free diving (breath holding) a man experiences changes in his buoyancy due to lung compression. A diver may start with positive buoyancy, change to neutral buoyancy due to lung compression, and then, if his lung volume is great enough and the dive is a deep one, he may experience negative buoyancy at depth.

A knowledge of the principles of buoyancy coupled with an understanding of Boyle's Law are needed when performing salvage work.

Heat

Heat is closely related to temperature, but different substances do not contain the same amount of heat at identical temperatures. Temperature is measured in degrees and is related to the energy content of the object, that is, a cubic foot of water will melt more ice than a cubic foot of air at the same temperature. Heat is measured in British thermal units (BTU) or in calories. One BTU is the amount of heat required to increase the temperature of one pint of water 1°F. One calorie is the amount of heat it takes to raise 1 gram of water 1°C.

Heat and temperature are important to the diver because in the water body heat is lost more rapidly than in air. Again, this is due to the greater energy of the water. The thermal conductivity of water is 20 times that of air. When man is immersed therefore he quite rapidly begins to lose body heat. To prevent heat loss by conduction the diver must wear such protective clothing as wet suits, dry suits, wet dry suits, or constant volume suits. In extremely cold water or when long immersions are required, it is desirous to circulate hot water through the suit. Although most heat loss in the water is through conduction, all three methods of heat transfer should be mentioned.

1. Conduction is the transmission directly from molecule to molecule.
2. Convection is the transmission of heat by the movement of heated gas or fluid.
3. Radiation is the transmission of heat in invisible waves. At sufficiently high temperature these waves produce light.

Light

We see as a result of the property of light as well as from physiological reasons. Light and its reflected colors and intensity produce visual images. In air we see by light rays being refracted by the cornea and focused on the retina.

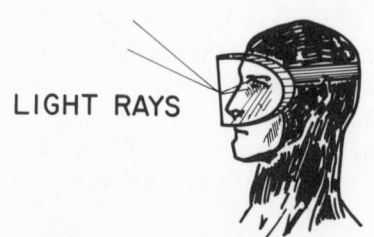

LIGHT RAYS

Fig. 3. The mask provides a necessary air space between eye and water for better visibility underwater.

Underwater, images we see appear to be blurred, and an air gap between the eye and the water must be established to have good vision. Due to refraction, however, objects appear to be magnified in the water by 25%.

Once light enters the water, visibility may be limited by absorption, scattering or diffusion of light rays, turbidity, and illumination. The depth of penetration of light waves varies considerably, but even in the clearest water photosynthesis cannot be maintained much below 650 feet.

Colors are absorbed as they pass through the water, and the order in which this absorption takes place is red, orange, yellow, green, blue, indigo, and violet. The exact depths where absorption of specific colors takes place vary somewhat with the water conditions present.

Sound

Sound originates from vibrating matter. To produce and hear sound, three things are required—a vibrating body, a transmitting medium, and a receiver (ear).

In air, sound travels at 1,090 feet per second, but in water the speed is accelerated to 4,700 feet per second. Due to this high velocity and because most sound energy is lost when being transmitted from air to water, it is difficult to communicate and to determine direction in the water by sound.

Review questions for chapter 1

1. Define physics.
2. What is the chemical composition of air?
3. Define the following:
   (a) pressure
   (b) kinetic theory of gases
   (c) atmospheric pressure
   (d) psi
   (e) psig
4. What is the density of salt water? Freshwater?
5. Define the following gas laws and explain the diving hazards and conditions to which each is most closely related.
   (a) Boyle's
   (b) Charles'
   (c) Dalton's
   (d) Henry's
   (e) Archimedes' Principle
6. A tank is charged to 2,985 psig at a temperature of 100°C. When the tank is used the air has cooled to 60°F. If a diver breathes .5 cubic feet

per minute, what is the maximum dive time he has at a depth of 67 feet, assuming that the tank he is using is rated at 100 cubic feet at a pressure of 2,800 psig?

7. What is the partial pressure for each gas listed at the depths indicated? The gas mixture is 10% O_2, 70% He, and 20% N_2.

Depth

97 feet	Helium	Nitrogen	Oxygen . . . . . .
133 feet	Helium	Nitrogen	Oxygen . . . . . .
231 feet	Helium	Nitrogen	Oxygen . . . . . .
421 feet	Helium	Nitrogen	Oxygen . . . . . .

8. A diver weighs 177 pounds and needs 10 pounds of weight for neutral buoyancy in salt water. How much salt water does he displace?

9. What effect does distortion of light have on the diver's vision?

10. What are the three requirements for producing and hearing sound?

11. List three ways in which heat is transmitted.

12. Explain why man is not crushed by the increased pressures encountered in diving.

13. A diver weighs 168 pounds and displaces 2 2/3 cubic feet. Will he float or sink in freshwater? In salt water?

14. An air compressor delivers 30 cubic feet of air at sea level. How many cubic feet will it deliver to ventilate the helmet of a diver at 300 feet?

15. The pressure exerted at sea level is ____ psi or ____ atm. or ____ mm Hg.

16. The partial pressure of oxygen (PO_2) at 297 feet in a mixture of 60% N_2, 30% He, and 10% O_2 is ____ psi; the percentage of N_2 is ____.

17. A double tank scuba unit provides an individual with 90 minutes of diving time at 33 feet. How long will the same unit last the diver at 165 feet?

18. Boyle's Law best explains ____ , ____ , and ____ .
    (a) air embolism
    (b) nitrogen narcosis
    (c) ear squeeze
    (d) oxygen toxicity
    (e) lung squeeze

19. The partial pressure of O_2 at a depth of 297 feet in a gas mixture of 20% N_2, 70% He, and 10% O_2 is ____; the percentage of He at the bottom is _____.

20. Pressure increase in seawater may be computed at the rate of ____ psi per foot of water depth.
    (a) .423

(b) .432

(c) .445

(d) .454

21. The pressure at a depth of 66 feet in seawater would be ____ psi.
    (a) 14.7
    (b) 30.0
    (c) 44.1
    (d) 63.4

22. A given volume of gas at the surface is reduced by ____ % when taken to 33 feet in salt water.
    (a) 100
    (b) 50
    (c) 30
    (d) 25

23. If a diver has a surface consumption rate of .5 cubic foot per minute, then 70 cubic feet of air will last him ____ minutes at 33 feet.
    (a) 25
    (b) 35
    (c) 60
    (d) 70

24. A pressure of 73.5 psi would be found at ____ feet of salt water.
    (a) 33
    (b) 66
    (c) 99
    (d) 132

25. Henry's Law deals with:
    (a) temperature
    (b) gas absorption
    (c) buoyancy
    (d) pressure and volume

26. As the partial pressure of a gas increases, the amount of gas which dissolves in a liquid
    (a) decreases
    (b) stays the same
    (c) increases

27. Partial pressures and oxygen toxicity can be used to explain why compressed air:
    (a) must be filtered before filling tanks
    (b) should not be used below 300 feet
    (c) exerts a greater pressure when heated

(d) should not be transported in an airplane

28. In most cases the buoyancy of the human body with lungs full of air is:
(a) positive
(b) negative
(c) neutral

29. If a square block of wood displaces 9 cubic feet and weighing 192 pounds were placed in salt water, it would
(a) sink
(b) float one half above the surface
(c) float two-thirds above the surface
(d) float one-third above the surface

30. A diver weighing 170 pounds and displacing 3 cubic feet of water would have to add _____ of lead weight to be neutrally buoyant in seawater? (Assume the volume of lead is zero.)
(a) 17 pounds
(b) 22 pounds
(c) 32 pounds
(d) 64 pounds

31. When seen from the surface a fish is not actually where it appears to be underwater due to:
(a) reflection
(b) refraction
(c) convection
(d) interference

32. Which of the following gases has a noticeable odor?
(a) nitrogen
(b) oxygen
(c) carbon dioxide
(d) carbon monoxide
(e) none of the above

33. Pressure increases at a rate of _____ psi per foot of freshwater depth.
(a) .423
(b) .432
(c) .445
(d) .454

2

Physiology

Upon entering the water, man is subjected to many physiological hazards. To prevent diving mishaps and maladies, man must understand their causes and effects, and must have a basic understanding of anatomy and physiology. The human body in operation is comparable to machinery, except that no machinery can duplicate all the complex functions of man. Many interrelated organs and systems make this complex system function. Proper function of these organs and systems is based on metabolism at the cellular level.

The major systems that enable the life cycle of man to continue are the skeletal system, the muscular system, the digestive system, the urinary system, the reproduction system, the endocrine system, the nervous system, the circulatory system, and the respiratory system. Although the life cycle depends on all these, as divers we are primarily concerned with the nervous system, the respiratory system, and the circulatory system. Proper function of these three systems is vital to divers, and anything affecting their normal functions will result in interference with the overall function of the body. Most diving maladies affect one or more of these systems, and thus a discussion of these systems and their basic functions is appropriate. The nervous system is responsible for enacting all reactions, and the respiratory and circulatory systems enable the process of metabolism to be carried out (see Figure 4).

Nervous System

The major responsibility of the nervous system is to control the functions and reactions of the body. To accomplish this, nervous impulses are sent out to the various organs and systems of the body, commanding them

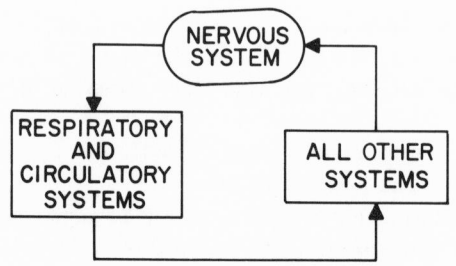

Fig. 4. Interactions of body systems.

to carry out a particular response. For simplicity's sake we will view the nervous system as composed of the

Central nervous system (CNS) which controls consciousness, mental activity, motor function, and skeletal muscles. The CNS consists of the brain and spinal cord.

Peripheral nervous system (PNS) which carries out the functions of the CNS. The PNS consists of the cranial and spinal nerves.

Autonomic nervous system, which controls man's internal environment and emotional reactions. Most of the centers controlling it are located within the CNS.

Anything that blocks or interferes with nerve transmission will affect the function of the body. Many diving maladies affect the nervous system and thus the symptoms appear to be quite similar. For instance, if the partial pressure of oxygen (PO_2) is too low, the brain becomes hypoxic; and if PO_2 is too high, the CNS is affected and produces symptoms varying from numbness to convulsions. If gas bubbles form, as in decompression sickness or air embolism, nerve transmission may be blocked or circulation cut off to parts of the nervous system, thus producing symptoms ranging from weakness to paralysis or even death.

Respiratory System

Respiration is the use of oxygen and the production of carbon dioxide and the exchange of these gases within the system. The respiratory system enables these functions to be accomplished. The nasal cavity, nasopharynx, larynx, trachea, bronchi, and lungs make up the respiratory system.

Essentially the respiratory system consists of moist and permeable membranes with a moving stream of blood. The membranes contain on one side a high PO_2 and on the other side a high PCO_2 (partial pressure of carbon dioxide).

The lungs are the primary organs of respiration and consist of the bronchial tubes, their terminal dilations the alveoli, blood vessels, lymphatics, and nerves. Air exchange takes place across air sacs referred to as alveoli.

The process of respiration is based on ventilation, moving air in and out (inspiration and expiration) or breathing.

For better understanding, respiration can be separated into two categories: external respiration or the exchange of gases in the lungs to the blood (breathing in and alveolar exchange), and internal respiration, which is the exchange of gases within the cells. Achievement of respiration requires a stimulus and a corresponding muscular response. Figure 5 shows the stimuli for respiration.

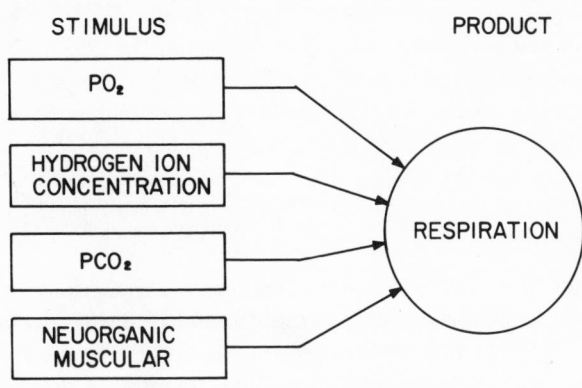

Fig. 5. Stimuli for respiration.

The respiratory center located in the medulla oblongata is triggered by one of several sources, and in return sends out nervous impulses to the respiratory muscles. Normally the primary stimulus to respiration is CO_2. The respiratory muscles consist of the following for inspiration: diaphragm, external intercostal muscles, the scaleni, sternocleidomastoid, pectorals minor, and the serratus posticus superior. Normally, expiration occurs as a passive act due to gravity and the elastic recoil of the lungs.

Normally, ventilation is caused by the respiratory center sending out nervous impulses to the diaphragm and adjusting respiratory depth and rhythm to body needs. In addition, respiration is stimulated by the lung reflex (Hering-Breuer reflex). Carbon dioxide is perhaps one of the strongest stimuli affecting breathing. Under normal conditions when breath holding, a strong urge to breathe occurs within 20 to 27 seconds due to a high

CO_2 buildup. Individuals not trained in breath-hold diving will notice this to be true when they are swimming underwater, for instance, when they attempt to swim across a pool on one breath. A block diagram representing normal respiration is given in Figure 6.

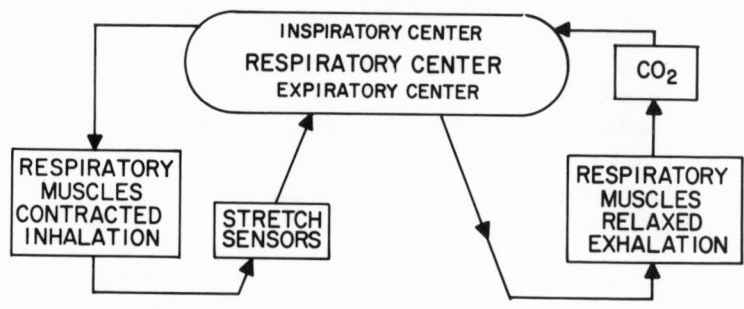

Fig. 6. Normal respiration.

It is perhaps easier to understand respiration if we break it into six steps: breathing, alveolar exchange, transport by blood, exchange to tissue fluids, exchange to cells, and metabolism. Breathing and alveolar exchange constitute external respiration, and the remaining steps represent internal respiration.

As has been discussed, the act of breathing is stimulated by the respiratory center. Gas exchange in the lungs takes place due to the process of diffusion. When oxygen enters the blood it is combined with hemoglobin and forms oxyhemoglobin, which is then transported throughout the body. Exchange of gases down to the cellular level also occurs through diffusion. At the cellular level during the process of metabolism oxygen combines with food and carbon dioxide is given off as a by-product. Due to metabolism we have energy, heat, waste, etc. The carbon dioxide is then returned by the blood to the lungs and exhaled in the same method as oxygen was brought to the cells (see Figure 7).

The amount of oxygen an individual uses is determined by his energy expenditure, body size, and circulatory factors. Normal respiration usually is at a rate of 12 to 20 times per minute at a volume of 500 cubic centimeters.

The capacities of the lungs can be discussed in the following terms.

Tidal air, which is the normal volume of air that moves in and out in a respiratory cycle.

Inspiratory reserve volume, the amount of air that can be inhaled at the end of normal inhalation.

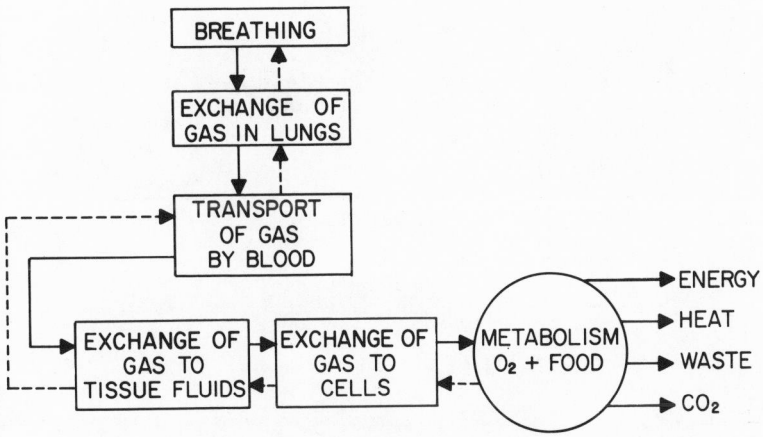

Fig. 7. Respiration in six steps.

Expiratory reserve volume, the amount of air that can be exhaled at the end of expiration.

Residual volume, the amount of air left in the lungs after forceful expiration.

Vital capacity, the amount of air that can be forcefully exhaled from a fully inflated lung.

Total lung volume, the total volume of gas in the lungs.

In diving certain maladies can and do affect the respiratory system. Some of these maladies are due to increased gas density, mechanical resistances, effects of increased partial pressures, and bubble formation due to improper ascent. Each of these maladies will be discussed in greater detail in the following chapters.

Circulatory System

The circulatory system is a closed loop system consisting of the heart, arteries, veins, tissue capillaries, and lung capillaries. The heart is the pump that propels the blood through the system (see Figure 8).

The force with which the heart propels blood is referred to as the blood pressure. Blood pressure depends upon the amount of blood being pumped and the resistance of the vessels through which it is pumped. The carotid sinuses are pressure-sensing devices that aid in controlling blood pressure by informing the brain, through nervous impulses, about pressures. The pulse indicates each time the heart beats, and the pulse rate varies from 80 beats per minute to over 150 during hard work. (In liters per minute of blood pumped, the variation is from 4 liters to 20 liters or an equivalent of

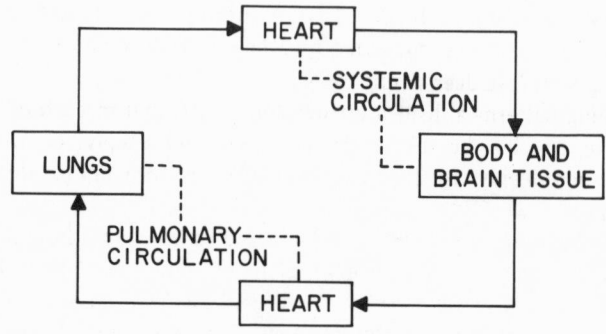

Fig. 8. Circulatory system.

up to 300 gallons an hour). The normal blood pressure at rest is approximately 120 mm Hg on contraction (systolic pressure) and about 80 mm Hg between beats (diastolic pressure). These pressures increase with age as the arteries lose elasticity.

Oxygen is combined with hemoglobin and carried by the red blood cells in blood. At normal PO_2 the hemoglobin carries about 98% of the oxygen it is capable of carrying. At the tissue level most of this oxygen is given up through diffusion and carbon dioxide is picked up.

The circulatory system can be further divided into the pulmonary and systemic systems, each of which has its own half of the heart for a pump and its own arteries and veins.

Figure 8 illustrates the operation of the circulatory system.

Anything that restricts or interferes with circulation will interfere with gas transport to and from the tissues. In diving, problems arise that can affect circulation, and sometimes protective clothing worn by the diver (such as an overly tight wet suit) may interfere with circulation. Most problems affecting circulation in diving are due to improper ascent rates or breath-holding ascents when using compressed air.

Breathing Resistance

Another area of interest to the diver is that of breathing resistance. It is obvious that if breathing resistance is too great, efficient ventilation cannot be maintained. A few factors that affect breathing are:

Dead spaces—areas where little or no gas exchange takes place (such as airways, snorkels, regulator mouthpieces, and full face masks).

Equipment resistance—equipment must be designed to allow ease in breathing and to insure sufficient volume of air, with no obstructions in the flow of this air.

Density—according to Boyle's Law, as pressure is increased so is density. Dense gas causes increased breathing resistance and is one of the limiting factors in deep diving using air.

Breathing pattern—a diver must develop an efficient method of ventilation; to do this, he must breathe slowly and deeply. By breathing slowly and deeply the diver avoids developing turbulent gas flow in his airways.

Gas flow in the airways can be compared to gas flow through a tube. Factors affecting gas flow are length, diameter, and rate of flow. In man, the airways are usually a constant length and diameter so our major concern is to control the rate of gas flow. The more rapid the breathing becomes, the more gas molecules bounce off the walls of the airways, thus causing resistance to ventilation. If respiration is slow and deep, the gas will tend to have a minimum of turbulence (see Figure 9).

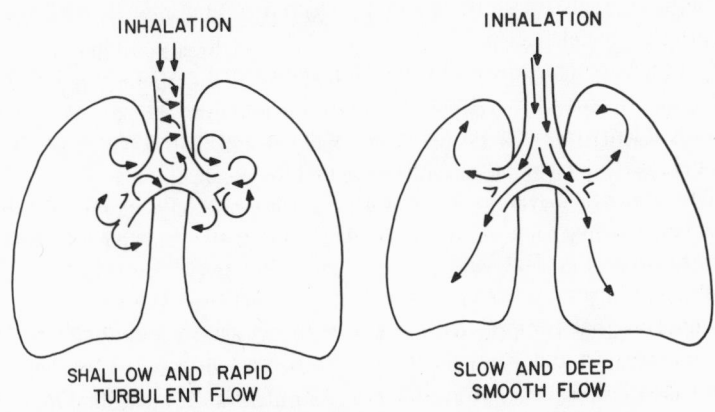

INHALATION

INHALATION

SHALLOW AND RAPID
TURBULENT FLOW

SLOW AND DEEP
SMOOTH FLOW

Fig. 9. Breathing resistance, shown on *left,* created by incorrect breathing pattern. *Right,* correct flow through airway.

Effective ventilation therefore requires forethought. Work loads should be limited, and heavy exertion should only be performed intermittently. Once a diver starts to become winded, he should stop physical activity and concentrate on reestablishing an efficient breathing pattern.

Oxygen and Carbon Dioxide Limits

To sustain life, oxygen must be transported and used in the body and carbon dioxide must be removed. When these gases vary greatly from their normal limits, the life processes may be threatened.

The partial pressure of oxygen determines whether or not the breathing medium is adequate. At sea level the partial pressure of oxygen represents approximately 21% of the gas. If the oxygen is allowed to drop to 16%, symptoms of hypoxia may develop; at about 10% most individuals will lose consciousness.

Percentages are based on 1 atm. of pressure. At higher pressures it is desirable to select a gas mixture that is the equivalent of 20 to 40% of 1 atm. The actual gas mixture on the surface may only be 2 to 10% oxygen, but when used at increased pressure the same mixture would be equivalent to 20% of surface volume. An increase to the equivalent of 60% of 1 atm. or above will result in lung damage, and increases to 100% and above may affect the central nervous system.

A high carbon dioxide level (hypercapnia) can cause symptoms similar to hypoxia. At 10% of 1 atm., consciousness is usually lost, and at approximately 15% muscular spasm and rigidity occur. Permanent brain damage is not as likely from hypercapnia as from hypoxia. Hypocapnia, or low carbon dioxide, may be produced by voluntary hyperventilation (over-breathing and blowing off CO_2, used to extend breath-holding ability) causing symptoms ranging from light-headedness and tingling to, in extreme cases, a nervous sensation of suffocation and even shock.

Hyperventilation may occur intentionally or unintentionally. Unintentional hyperventilation is usually triggered by nervous tension and can occur to anyone under stress. This reaction may be very subtle, and the individual may not be aware of its development at first. This phenomena is probably responsible for many drownings among divers, and it frequently precedes panic.

In many cases if a diver who is working hard or in a stressful situation (even including overdetermination to accomplish some act) stops at the first sign of feeling uncomfortable and concentrates on breathing, he will find that he has started to hyperventilate. If he begins breathing correctly, the uncomfortable feeling will pass. Unchecked hyperventilation in diving causes turbulent air flow adding to breathing resistance. Thus a whole chain of events begins that may lead to an accident.

Intentional hyperventilation is employed frequently by breath-holding divers. The advantages are obvious: by blowing off CO_2 the breath-holding time is increased. When done in excess, however, it is possible for the diver, during ascent, to lose consciousness from hypoxia.

Carbon Monoxide

Carbon monoxide (CO), a by-product of combustion, can produce harmful effects if breathed. Carbon monoxide can be picked up by the air compressor and pumped to a diver's air supply. To avoid this happening, the compressor intake must be isolated from gas engines and other sources of CO.

Carbon monoxide is deadly because it combines with hemoglobin 200 times as readily as oxygen. The hemoglobin, therefore, loses its affinity for oxygen, and the diver ceases to receive adequate oxygen. Individuals with CO poisoning will characteristically have red lips and symptoms of hypoxia.

Hypoglycemia

Hypoglycemia is low blood sugar. Sugar (glucose) is the main fuel of the body, and if hypoglycemia is present the functions of the tissues will be interrupted. The brain is especially sensitive to hypoglycemia. Some of the symptoms are weakness, dizziness, confusion, lack of coordination, and unusual hunger, symptoms similar to those of decompression sickness. Divers may feel similar symptoms if they have neglected to eat sufficiently.

Man depends upon proper functioning of his internal systems for his overall health and well-being. Any abnormality of these systems results in physiological reactions. As mentioned previously most of the processes of circulation and respiration are dependent upon pressures and partial pressures. When man descends into the water his tissues absorb gases at an increased partial pressure. The effects of these gases can produce severe physiological reactions if not understood and compensated for or avoided.

Review questions for chapter 2

1. List the major body systems.
2. Which three major systems are of prime concern to divers?
3. List the three divisions of the nervous system and tell what each consists of.
4. Human respiration may best be defined as
   (a) use of carbon dioxide and production of oxygen and the exchange of these gases within the system
   (b) use of nitrogen for control of respiration
   (c) use and transport of all inert gas
   (d) absorption and elimination of inert gas
   (e) use of oxygen and production of carbon dioxide and the exchange of these gases within the system
   (f) all of the above

5. Define:
   (a) External respiration
   (b) Internal respiration

6. The terminal ends of the bronchial tubes are the _____, and their function is to _____ .

7. Arrange the following to reflect the stimulation and production of respiration. Explain the process of respiration.
   (a) CO_2
   (b) Respiratory muscles
   (c) Stretch sensors
   (d) Muscular effort inhalation
   (e) Respiratory center
   (f) Elastic recoil exhalation

8. List six steps in the process of respiration.

9. The circulatory system is a closed loop system consisting of_____

10. What is blood pressure?

11. Define the following:
    (a) Respiratory cycle
    (b) Respiratory rate
    (c) Total lung capacity
    (d) Vital capacity
    (e) Tidal air
    (f) Inspiratory reserve volume
    (g) Expiratory reserve volume
    (h) Residual volume
    (i) Respiratory minute volume
    (j) Maximum breathing capacity
    (k) Respiratory dead space
    (l) Net alveolar ventilation

12. Explain the term pulse rate.

13. Lack of oxygen results in
    (a) hypocapnia
    (b) hypercapnia
    (c) hyperoxia
    (d) hypoxia

14. Diagram the circulatory system and explain how oxygen gets to the tissue level.

15. Diving equipment that contributes to the problem of respiratory dead spaces are _____ and _____ .

16. Explain the effect of turbulent air flow on a diver.

17. Two circuits that make up the circulatory system are _____
    and _____.
18. Which of the following components transport oxygen throughout the
    system?
    (a) Lymph
    (b) Red blood cells
    (c) White blood cells
    (d) Platelets
19. Carbon monoxide combines with hemoglobin approximately
    _____times as readily as oxygen.
20. The minimum percentage of oxygen necessary to support life at sea
    level is
    (a) 20%
    (b) 16%
    (c) 14%
    (d) 10%
21. Define hypoglycemia.
22. The amount of carbon dioxide lost by the blood depends mainly on
    (a) partial pressure of the carbon dioxide
    (b) amount of plasma in the blood
    (c) amount of serum in the blood
    (d) amount of hemoglobin in the blood
23. Alcohol causes
    (a) the speed-up of the circulatory system
    (b) circulatory depression
    (c) improved response to sudden occurrences
    (d) an increase in body temperature
24. The amount of air in the lungs that cannot be blown out no matter
    how hard the diver tries is
    (a) residual volume
    (b) complementary volume
    (c) supplementary volume
    (d) tidal air
25. Hyperventilation prolongs breath holding by
    (a) increasing the alveolar partial pressure of O_2
    (b) increasing the cerebral partial pressure of O_2
    (c) decreasing the alveolar partial pressure of CO_2
    (d) decreasing chest and diaphragm reflexes
    (e) satisfying the cerebral impulse to inhale a specific volume of air
    each minute

3

Barotrauma

When man is subjected to increased pressure, the air spaces in his body offer potential sites of injury. Barotrauma means pressure injury. The areas of greatest concern are the ears, the sinuses, the lungs, and associated airways.

During descent these air spaces are subjected to compression and on ascent decompression (expansion). Because the effects of increased and decreased pressures affect the diver differently, our discussion will be broken into descent problems and ascent problems.

Descent Problems

During descent the diver is subjected to compression of air spaces as described in Boyle's Law (PV = K). When related to the middle ear space, sinuses, or lungs, this means being "squeezed," and the effects are illustrated in Figure 10.

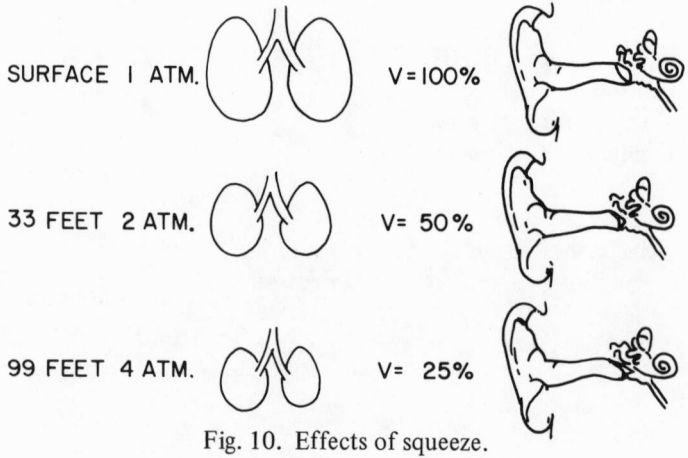

SURFACE I ATM.   V = 100%

33 FEET 2 ATM.   V = 50%

99 FEET 4 ATM.   V = 25%

Fig. 10. Effects of squeeze.

The principal parts of the ear are the outer ear, the eardrum, the middle ear, the inner ear, and the eustachian tube (see Figure 11).

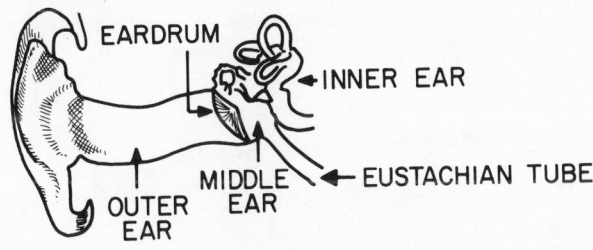

Fig. 11. Principal parts of the ear.

When environmental pressure is increased, the pressure exerts force against the flexible membrane material of the eardrum. The reaction of the drum then is to be pressed inward, producing symptoms of discomfort and pain. If more pressure increase is experienced, blood fluids exude into the middle ear and the eardrum finally ruptures (see Figure 12), allowing water to enter the middle ear.

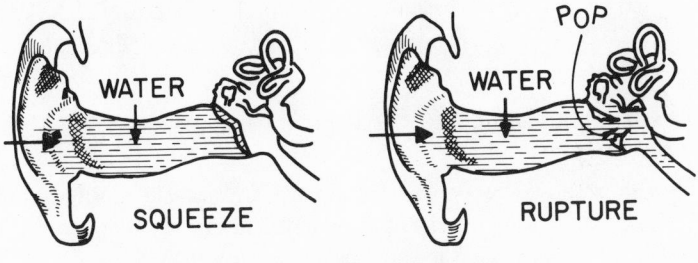

Fig. 12. Pressure in the ear creates squeeze,
which can rupture the eardrum.

Ear squeeze is prevented by allowing pressure to be put into the middle air space so that it is equal to the atmospheric pressure. This pressure must pass from the mouth through the eustachian tube and is built up by swallowing, closing off the nostrils and lightly blowing or yawning, and in some individuals by wiggling the jaws. This equalization is almost automatic in some individuals but in others equalization procedures must be performed constantly. It is common for novice divers to take three to five minutes to equalize their ears to a depth of 33 feet. However, most people, if they "keep up" with the equalization process, can descend fairly fast. The term keeping up does not imply equalizing the ears when one feels pain. Pain indicates that the squeeze is already present. Equalization should begin the instant descent is started and must be performed continually so that the squeeze condition is avoided. Many divers "pop" (simulate equalization) their ears on the surface and if using a descending line (line from the boat to ocean floor) equalize their ears each time they change hand positions during descent (see Figure 13).

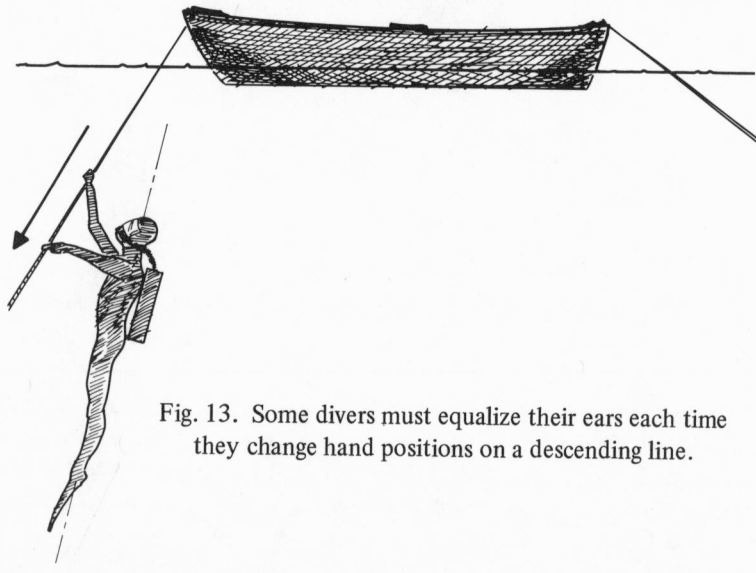

Fig. 13. Some divers must equalize their ears each time they change hand positions on a descending line.

As with most things, experience in equalization usually results in fewer problems. Repeated use of equalization methods conditions the muscles at the base of the eustachian tube and makes the process easier and faster.

If the diver fails to equalize the pressure in his ears and the eardrum ruptures, the immediate sensations are dizziness, nausea, and disorientation. These symptoms result from cold water entering the middle ear. When this happens the diver should attempt to remain in one position by holding onto something. Once the water reaches body temperature, the symptoms will probably disappear or diminish. He should then, of course, exit the water. After an eardrum is ruptured there is a great chance of infection so the diver should seek medical attention and be placed on antihistamines and antibiotics.

Another source of ear discomfort experienced by divers is outer ear infection (fungus or bacteria). Proper care of the ears will help prevent infections. Objects, even fingers and sterile swabs should not be placed in the outer ear. Persons who are prone to ear infections or people spending several hours per day in the water should use an artificial lubricant (olive oil, baby oil, etc.) and apply a preventative solution, such as Domeboro solution, to their ears at the end of the diving day. Another good practice is to dry the ears with a hair dryer. Extensive use of alcohol in the ears should be avoided.

The sinuses represent another common area of squeeze. The diver is concerned with four sinuses: frontals, ethmoidal, maxillary, and sphenoid (see Figure 14).

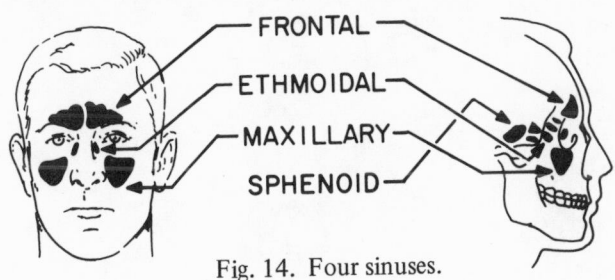

FRONTAL
ETHMOIDAL
MAXILLARY
SPHENOID

Fig. 14. Four sinuses.

Symptoms from sinus squeeze will be pain or numbness and will depend on which sinuses are affected. A diver with a cold may have difficulty equalizing his sinuses. Equalization of the sinuses is achieved in the same method as equalization of the ear. Afrin or other nasal sprays may be used to expedite equalization, but these should only be used if absolutely necessary. Strong decongestants or antihistamines should be avoided when diving due to their effect on diver behavior (dizziness, etc.).

The lungs of a breath-holding diver (free diver) also are compressed as he descends. Thus he experiences a change in buoyancy. In theory the possibility of lung squeeze exists, yet much of the recent work in the field creates doubt as to exactly when or if a lung squeeze does occur.

Ascent Problems

According to Boyle's Law, if the pressure is reduced, the volume will be increased. If we apply this statement to a diver who is breathing air at a depth of 99 feet, we will see that as he ascends he will be traveling from 4 atm. to 1 atm. of pressure. If during this ascent he closes his airways (fails to breathe or exhale), then his lungs will double their volume between 99 feet and 33 feet and then double again between 33 feet and the surface. It is apparent then that something will "give" due to these volumetric changes. The lungs in this case would rupture (see Figure 15).

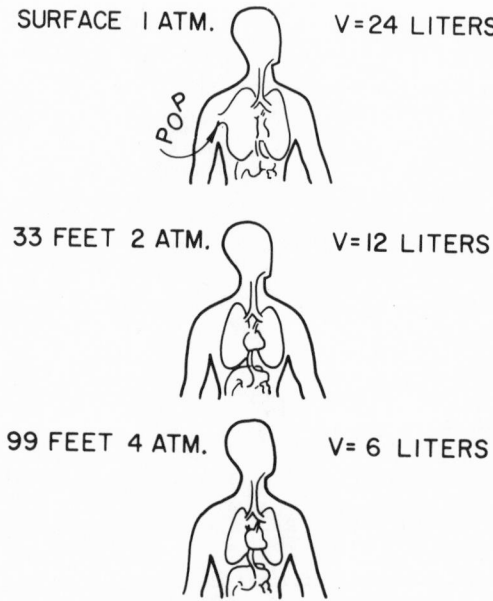

SURFACE 1 ATM. V = 24 LITERS

33 FEET 2 ATM. V = 12 LITERS

99 FEET 4 ATM. V = 6 LITERS

Fig. 15. Lungs in the top illustration ruptured
because of pressure changes during faulty ascent.

Rupturing of the lungs can result in one or more of the following:

Air embolism
Pneumothorax
Interstitial emphysema (subcutaneous and mediastinal emphysema)

The most serious of these problems is air embolism, especially cerebral air embolism. Mechanically, as the diver ascends holding his breath, his lungs are overexpanded. This results in stretching and tearing of the alveoli. When the alveoli are torn, gas can escape into the pulmonary circulation in the form of bubbles. These bubbles are then carried through the heart and pumped to the brain and throughout the body. Many of the bubbles will lodge in blood vessels and therefore cut off or reduce blood flow to the tissues beyond that point. The effect of this blockage is to remove or reduce available oxygen to the affected tissues. Results are obvious—the tissue becomes hypoxic and starts to die or is damaged. The brain, of course, is most susceptible to hypoxia and will experience permanent damage within minutes. Cerebral air embolism is characterized by symptoms of blurry vision, blindness, unconsciousness, and loss of motor function. If the bubbles lodge in the spinal cord, there will be paralysis or staggers. Other symptoms of air embolism depend on the exact bubble location (see Figure 16).

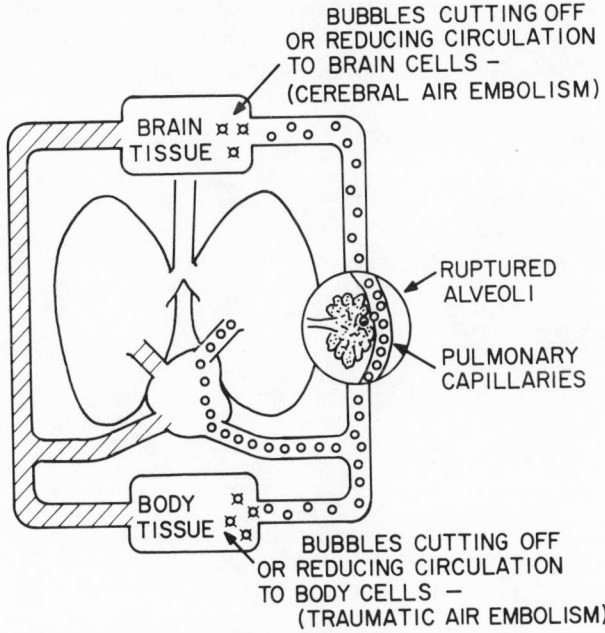

Fig. 16. Air embolism.

A classical case of air embolism would be: a diver panics, holds his breath, and begins ascent; as the volume of his lungs is increased, pulmonary circulation is reduced and the alveoli are torn. Upon surfacing the diver exhales, thus reducing internal pressure of the lungs. Pulmonary circulation is restored, and air bubbles enter the systemic circulation. The diver's head is out of the water, bubbles are trapped in the blood vessels supplying the brain, and the diver loses consciousness due to loss of circulation (oxygen) to the brain.

Symptoms of air embolism will generally occur within five minutes of surfacing. This is the most serious accident that can occur to a diver, but it is the easiest to prevent. Prevention is simple: allow air to be vented during ascent by breathing normally or exhaling.

The first aid for air embolism is to place the diver on a tilt board or elevate his feet, left lateral side down; observe for shock; and administer mouth to mouth resuscitation if necessary.

The treatment for air embolism is prompt recompression at a facility having a recompression chamber. At this facility the diver will be recompressed to a depth of 165 feet and a lengthy treatment table must be followed. Under no conditions should the diver be placed in the water for treatment. In the water the exposure is too great and there is a possibility of drowning or inadequate treatment that might complicate final treatment.

Pneumothroax in divers is due to failure to breathe normally or exhale during ascent. Mechanically what happens is that the lung ruptures, allowing air to enter the pleural cavity. Normally there is a slightly negative intrathoracic pressure, but when air escapes a positive pressure exists and results in partially or totally collapsing the affected lung (see Figure 17).

PNEUMOTHORAX

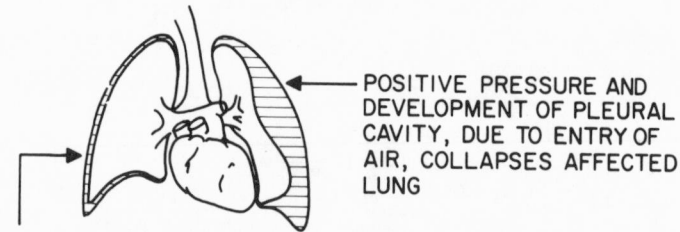

POSITIVE PRESSURE AND DEVELOPMENT OF PLEURAL CAVITY, DUE TO ENTRY OF AIR, COLLAPSES AFFECTED LUNG

NORMAL: SLIGHT NEGATIVE PRESSURE EXISTS DUE TO PLEURAL FLUID

Fig. 17. Pneumothorax.

Symptoms of pneumothorax may include severe chest pain and difficulty in breathing. This condition is avoided by breathing normally or exhaling during ascent.

First aid for pneumothorax is to observe for shock and to keep the patient comfortable until he arrives at a medical facility. Treatment includes surgical removal of the air and observation of the patient for more serious symptoms. If symptoms of air embolism develop, then the patient must be treated in a recompression chamber.

Interstitial emphysema occurs when bubbles enter the lung, rupture, and escape into the tissues. When the bubbles lodge in the tissues of the area of the mediastinum (see Figure 18), the occurrence is called mediastinal emphysema; in subcutaneous emphysema the bubbles usually lodge at the base of the neck and can frequently be felt and observed. Symptoms may be a difficulty in swallowing or breathing or a feeling of heartburn or chest pressure.

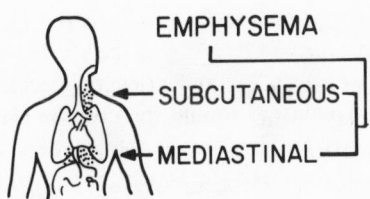

Fig. 18. Emphysema.

First aid and treatment consist of observing the patient for more serious symptoms. Frequently, when any of these conditions exist, the patient is treated by recompression as a safety precaution against air embolism.

Review questions for chapter 3

1. List three natural air spaces of the body and explain the occurrence of squeeze.
2. "Squeeze" occurs
   (a) only when free diving
   (b) only when scuba diving
   (c) only in the air pockets of the body
   (d) all the above
3. Draw and label the ear.
4. Draw and label the sinuses.
5. List three methods of equalizing the ears.
6. Give the cause, prevention, symptoms, and treatment of each of the following:
   (a) air embolism
   (b) pneumothorax
   (c) mediastinal emphysema
   (d) subcutaneous emphysema
7. Barotrauma refers to
   (a) ascent problems
   (b) descent problems
   (c) all pressure injuries
   (d) all diving problems
8. A scuba diver who surfaces, exhales, and passes out is most likely suffering from:
   (a) pneumothorax
   (b) air embolism
   (c) latent anoxia
   (d) decompression illness

9. Pneumothorax is caused by
   (a) air around the heart
   (b) lumps around the neck
   (c) air in the bloodstream
   (d) air between chest wall and lung

10. Draw a diagram showing the occurrence of air embolism.

11. Draw a diagram showing subcutaneous and mediastinal emphysema.

12. Subcutaneous emphysema is:
    (a) air around the heart
    (b) nitrogen under the skin around the base of the neck
    (c) aeroembolism
    (d) air under the skin around the base of the neck

13. The lung collapses, causing interference with breathing, in the condition known as:
    (a) air embolism
    (b) mediastinal emphysema
    (c) subcutaneous emphysema
    (d) pneumothorax

14. The most obvious symptom of pneumothorax is:
    (a) difficulty in breathing
    (b) lumps around the neck
    (c) difficulty in swallowing
    (d) bloody froth at the mouth

15. From the time of injury, symptoms of air embolism generally occur within
    (a) 5 minutes
    (b) 15 minutes
    (c) 30 minutes
    (d) 60 minutes

16. Pneumothorax, mediastinal emphysema, and subcutaneous emphysema are all caused by
    (a) going too deep
    (b) too rapid ascent
    (c) ascent while holding breath with scuba
    (d) staying down too long

17. A diver who is unconscious immediately after surfacing would be presumed to have which of the following maladies?
    (a) pneumothorax
    (b) air embolism
    (c) nitrogen narcosis

    (d) anoxia

    (e) decompression sickness

18. If equalization gets behind the rate of descent _____ may occur
    (a) air embolism
    (b) middle ear squeeze
    (c) inner ear squeeze
    (d) pneumothorax

19. Lung squeeze occurs most commonly in
    (a) scuba diving
    (b) skin diving
    (c) hard-hat diving
    (d) dry suit diving

20. Assuming a skin diver's residual lung volume is 2 pints and his total lung capacity is 17 pints, how deep can this diver dive (without any additional source of air) before a lung squeeze would be imminent?
    (a) 99 feet
    (b) 198 feet
    (c) 264 feet
    (d) no limit

21. Pain in an upper tooth during a dive most probably would be caused by
    (a) mask squeeze
    (b) an ethmoid sinus squeeze
    (c) a maxillary sinus squeeze
    (d) clenching the teeth too tightly

22. One should begin equalizing
    (a) immediately upon submerging
    (b) when the ears being to pain
    (c) at 33 feet
    (d) after the sinus cavities clear

23. Air forced into the space occupied by the heart and great vessels is termed
    (a) mediastinal emphysema
    (b) pneumothorax
    (c) air embolism
    (d) subcutaneous emphysema

24. Pneumothorax is a term referring to the collection of air
    (a) between the lung and the chest wall
    (b) between the middle and outer ear
    (c) between the lungs and blood vessels
    (d) between the ribs and the skin

25. A ruptured tympanic membrane can cause
    (a) severe pain in the sinus cavities
    (b) severe pain in the chest cavity
    (c) vertigo
    (d) cramps
26. Mask squeeze will occur if
    (a) you do not swallow
    (b) you do not equalize pressure in the ears
    (c) you do not exhale into the mask
    (d) you go to the surface too rapidly

4

Physiological Problems from Increased Partial Pressures

High partial pressures of oxygen and nitrogen and other so-called inert gases cause specific problems for the diver. Dalton's Law of partial pressures and Henry's Law of solubility give the foundation for an understanding of oxygen poisoning and inert gas narcosis.

Oxygen Poisoning

Oxygen is required for the life processes to continue; however, when the PO_2 is much above .4 atm. oxygen becomes a cellular toxin. Convulsions associated with high PO_2 indicating central nervous system involvement were described by Paul Bert in 1878; lung irritation was described by Lorraine Smith in 1899. Further investigation has revealed that there are two types of oxygen poisoning—chronic (low pressure) and acute. Sometimes these are identified as Lorraine Smith and Paul Bert effects.

Chronic oxygen poisoning occurs when man is exposed to a PO_2 of .6 to 2 atm. or 500 to 1,200 mm Hg. The PO_2 in these ranges act as an irritant to lung tissue, causing inflammation, congestion, hemorrhage, thickening of the walls of pulmonary arteries, and swelling of alveolar walls. These effects, of course, are dependent not only on the PO_2 but also on the duration of the exposure.

In studies on humans it was found that man could tolerate 12 hours at a PO_2 of 1 atm. prior to the onset of symptoms, and when the PO_2 was increased to 2 atm., pulmonary irritation was observed in 3 hours. At a PO_2 of 2 atm., pulmonary irritation was observed after 9 hours. Vital capacity was reduced by 90%. This reduction took 12 days to return to normal. Other symptoms of chronic oxygen poisoning are shortness of breath, dry cough, and fatigue.

Perhaps chronic oxygen poisoning can be better understood through knowledge of the surface active material in the lungs. The alveoli tend to collapse due to their physical properties. Collapse, however, is prevented by a lining of lipo protein material. This material lowers the surface tension of the lungs, stabilizing the alveoli and ensuring normal respiration. This low surface tension also prevents transudation from the capillaries, which would occur otherwise. If the amount of lung surfactant is decreased, a corresponding rise in alveolar surface tension may cause collapse of the alveoli. So, alterations of the surfactant due to increased PO_2 may be one of the underlying mechanisms of chronic oxygen poisoning.

Chronic oxygen poisoning becomes a factor worthy of consideration during saturation diving and prolonged treatment of diving disorders. Recent work by Dr. William Fife of Texas A & M University suggests that man may adapt to a limited degree of chronic oxygen poisoning. This work is based on experiments performed during dives on the saturation project hydrolab. Dr. Fife found while performing two missions back to back (14 days) using air at a depth of 42 feet of salt water (PO_2 of approximately .46 atm.) that during the first 4 to 6 days he had the anticipated reduction in pulmonary function expected. After 7 days, however, these effects began to reverse themselves. It is hoped that further work will be done along these lines.

In deeper saturation dives, chronic oxygen poisoning is avoided by using gas mixtures yielding a surface equivalent of approximately .21 atm. Treatment tables are designed so that acceptable concentrations of oxygen are not exceeded.

Acute oxygen poisoning is a problem peculiar to deep diving on gas mixtures using a high PO_2 or using oxygen rebreathers below 25 feet. Symptoms of oxygen poisoning may occur suddenly and without warning.

It has been demonstrated that there is a great variation in tolerances of acute oxygen poisoning among individuals, and that even an individual's tolerance may vary daily. Another discovery was that symptoms occur more rapidly in water than in a chamber, and that work further reduces tolerance.

Acute oxygen poisoning affects the nervous system and can produce one or all of the following symptoms: nausea, muscular twitching, dizziness, choking, and convulsion followed by loss of consciousness.

The mechanics of oxygen poisoning are not fully understood, but research has shown that several interacting problems aid in producing symptoms. Blood and circulation are affected, and increased PO_2 is followed by blood pressure and pulse drop. At a PO_2 of 1 atm., there is a 13% decrease in cerebral blood flow, and at a PO_2 of 3.5 atm. a 25%

decrease in cerebral blood flow has been observed. Cerebral vasocon-striction occurs due to arterial hypocapnia that accompanies the respi-ratory stimulation produced by oxygen. High PO_2 inhibits enzyme sys-tems (most enzymes containing sulfhydryl groups are inactivated by high PO_2 due to oxidation of these groups). Interference with functioning of electron transfer pathways and oxidative phosphorylation has been de-scribed by Chance, Jamieson, and Williamson (1966). In the brain, amino-butyric acid (GABA, an amino acid) is active in oxidative metabolism of the brain and acts as a depressant in nerve transmission and is believed to act as a modulator or inhibitory transmitter in the CNS. At high PO_2 there is a reduction in GABA. It has been shown that high GABA levels prevent convulsion and that convulsion can occur when low GABA levels are pre-sent.

Clearly more than one mechanism is responsible for the convulsions observed in acute oxygen poisoning. Awareness of the potential problems of the effects of high PO_2 is the key to avoidance. Acute oxygen poisoning is avoided by simply not exceeding a PO_2 of 1.8 atm. In air diving this would be equivalent to a depth of 9 atm. or 264 feet of salt water (FSW). This is the maximum PO_2 limit acceptable for work, and probably the depth should be limited to 240 FSW. This limit does not mean it is safe to make air dives to 240 FSW, as it is not; the limit is only significant as an illustration of the highest PO_2 acceptable.

High PO_2 can produce undesirable effects when certain limits are ex-ceeded. Many disease and diving illnesses, however, respond well to ele-vated PO_2 under controlled conditions. Oxygen therapy and hyperbaric medicine are valuable treatment assets to many of the disorders of man.

Inert Gas Narcosis

Inert gas narcosis, commonly called "nitrogen narcosis," has been defined in many ways. Bennett (1966) described it in connection with the Greek word nark. Nark means numbness and was originally used to describe the reactions produced by opium. Opium when swallowed, breathed, or in-jected produces stupification, drowsiness, or insensibility. Thus narcosis may be compared to an opium high. In the United States it is common to compare narcosis with alcohol intoxication (Martini's Law: 50 feet of descent is equivalent to one martini on an empty stomach) with symptoms of drowsiness, numbness, impaired motor function, etc. A simple defini-tion of nitrogen narcosis is that it is the intoxicating effect of nitrogen at high pressures.

The effects of narcosis are best explained by the Meyer-Overton hypothesis: Any inert substance will act as a depressant to the nervous system provided a sufficient quantity goes into solution in the lipid phase. A depressant action will be exerted by a gas in direct proportion to the amount that goes into solution. Originally the gas is dissolved in the blood; it is then transported to the tissue level where it may be distributed between the aqueous and fatty tissue per its partition coefficient. (The partition coefficient is the ratio of distribution between water and fat.) The narcotic effect of a gas is determined by multiplying the solubility by the partition coefficient (see Table 3).

Table 3. Narcotic Effects of Various Gases

Gas	Solubility*	Partition coefficient[†]	Potency[‡]
Nitrous oxide	0.549	3.2	1.76
Krypton	0.051	9.6	0.49
Argon	0.029	5.3	0.15
Nitrogen	0.013	5.2	0.068
Hydrogen	0.016	3.1	0.048
Helium	0.0085	1.7	0.014

* Measured in ml gms / ml water at $37°$ C.
† Ratio of gas in oil to gas in water.
‡ Solubility x partition coefficient.

Table 3 shows that nitrous oxide appears to be the least desirable gas and that helium appears to be the most desirable.

Due to the narcotic effect of nitrogen or other inert gases, depth limitations are placed on their use in diving. It is important that the diver be aware of narcosis and understand its effects from the subtle onset to the more serious symptoms.

As early as 1835 it was observed by Junod that breathing compressed air at depth caused symptoms of intoxication and a lively imagination. Further experimentation in 1861 by Green noted poor judgment and drowsiness at 160 feet. In 1939 Damant reported memory defects when men were compressed to 300 feet.

One of the more significant early experiments was conducted by Shilling and Willgrube in 1937. In their experiment 46 subjects were observed and tested at depths ranging from 90 to 300 feet. Some of the results of this experiment are shown in Table 4.

Table 4. Results of Shilling-Willgrube Experiment

Characteristic	Depth					
	0	100	150	200	250	300
Mean extra time to solve problems (sec)	0.35	6.89	9.74	13.98	26.07	31.42
Mean extra errors in problem solving	0.18	0.49	0.72	1.22	2.18	3.02
Mean decreased numbers crossed out		0.09	−2.30	−2.55	−5.85	−8.74
Average reaction time (sec)	0.214		0.237	.242	0.248	2.257
Mean extra time to solve problems (acclimated divers)	1.64	3.42	4.66	11.75	16.33	24.36

The Shilling and Willgrube experiment concluded that there is much individual variation and that experienced divers and individuals of high intelligence have a greater tolerance to narcosis.

In 1963 Kiessling and Magg utilized the Purdue pegboard to measure choice reaction time and to test conceptual reasoning. They found that at 100 feet reaction time decreased by 20.85%; mechanical dexterity decreased by 7.90%; and conceptual reasoning decreased by 33.46%. From these results it was concluded that mental function is the area most severely affected.

Early tests of manual skill and intellectual ability in depths between 250 and 300 feet were conducted by Case and Haldane. The conclusions from these tests were that narcosis primarily affected moral and intellectual performance.

Recent studies related in personal communication by Glen Egstrom of the University of California at Los Angeles indicate that narcosis effects begin as soon as man is exposed to slight pressure increases.

The exact mechanisms of inert gas narcosis are not understood, and as in oxygen poisoning many factors overlap to produce the narcosis. A few contributing factors are carbon dioxide retention, density of breathing mixture, alcohol, anxiety, fatigue, and temperature. In general, divers at 100 to 200 feet may experience lightheadedness, loss of fine discrimination, and euphoria, while at 200 to 250 feet they may experience poor judgment, slow reflexes, and peripheral numbness. Dives below 250 feet are considered extremely hazardous, and reliable tolerances for working much below 200 feet are seldom developed.

Perhaps the greatest danger of narcosis is not the obvious but the subtle symptom, such as changes in depth perception and unnoticed slowing of reflexes. Another consideration is that the narcosis may not be as great a threat to the diver himself as to the safety of his buddy. Slow reactions to a stressful incident could mean the difference between the easy handling of a problem or having an accident. From practical experience it is suggested that working dives below 200 feet be performed on mixed gases.

In summary, both oxygen poisoning and inert gas narcosis are produced by high partial pressures of the respective gases. The obvious solution to this problem is to avoid deep dives on air. We must also be aware that the nervous system is affected in both of these maladies and that it is easy to lose motor control or reasoning ability under the influence of these gases.

Review questions for chapter 4

1. Explain "chronic" oxygen poisoning.
2. What area is most susceptible to "low pressure" (chronic or Lorraine Smith effect) oxygen poisoning?
3. In what diving situations would chronic oxygen poisoning be a major danger?
4. List the symptoms of acute (high pressure) oxygen poisoning.
5. Give three contributing factors to acute oxygen poisoning.
6. How does one prevent oxygen poisoning?
7. Define nitrogen narcosis.
8. What action does narcosis have on the central nervous system?
9. Define the Meyer-Overton theory.
10. Circle true statements concerning nigrogen narcosis.
    (a) Nitrogen acts as a stimulant on the CNS.
    (b) Nitrogen at high partial pressures has an intoxicating effect on man.
    (c) Nitrogen acts as a depressant on the CNS.
    (d) Nitrogen acts as a stimulant on the respiratory center.
11. List three contributory factors to inert gas narcosis.
12. In what depth range do nitrogen narcosis symptoms normally become noticeable?
    (a) 0 to 50 feet
    (b) 50 to 100 feet
    (c) 100 to 150 feet
    (d) 150 to 200 feet

5

Decompression Sickness

Decompression sickness is, as the name implies, a disease associated with improper decompression. The term decompression refers to ascending from a given pressure to a lower pressure; in other words, improper decompression could be expressed as improper ascent. In the act of traveling from a high pressure to a low pressure, the tissues and blood give off gas or, in other words, they enter a degassing phase.

For understanding problems that occur due to improper decompression, it is helpful to review some basic concepts of physics and physiology. When man is exposed to pressure, whether it be 1 atm. or 10 atm., his body will tend to take up gases at their respective partial pressures dependent upon their solubility. At sea level the partial pressure of nitrogen which the tissues are exposed is .79 atm., and the amount in solution is dependent upon the solubility of the specific tissues. When man is compressed to 10 atm., his environmental pressure greatly exceeds tissue pressure, and thus the process of diffusion is speeded up. According to Henry's Law, the amount of gas that will go into solution is almost proportional to the partial pressure of that gas. We can see that the term almost is used to illustrate both the solubility of a particular tissue and the time factor, the rate at which the tissues become saturated. Considering these facts, it is obvious that at 10 atm. the maximum partial pressure of nitrogen would be .79 x 10 or 7.9 atm. Tissue equilibrium is attained through the processes of diffusion dependent upon the respiratory and circulatory systems. In other words the diver breathes the gas in; there is an exchange of gas in the lungs; the gas is transported by the blood, allowing an exchange to tissue fluids, and then exchanged to the cells. From these steps we can see that the increased gas tension in the blood is carried to the tissue level and then to the cells. The blood can carry only a certain threshold of gas and thus it will take many cycles of circulation (or time) to achieve equilibrium (see Figure 19).

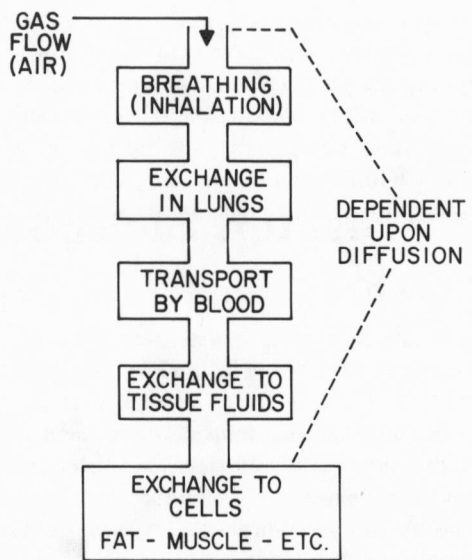

Fig. 19. Diagram showing gas carried throughout body during descent.

The reverse process holds true on ascent, when the tissues have a greater gas pressure than the external pressure. Then gas diffuses out of the tissues and is carried by the blood back to the lungs where it is vented off (see Figure 20).

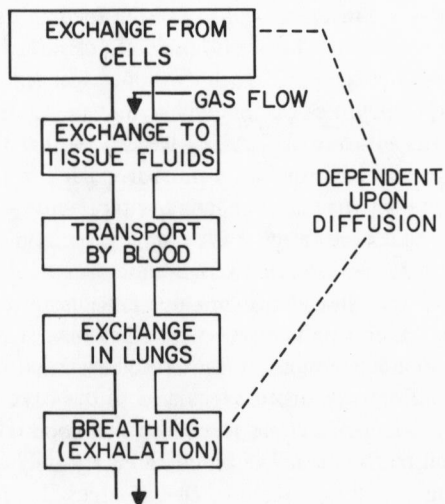

Fig. 20. Diagram showing gas given off by lungs during ascent.

Decompression sickness occurs when the ascent rate (rate at which pressure changes are made) is faster than the ability of the body tissues and blood to keep the gas in solution and venting off at an even rate, thus producing bubbles. When bubble size is large enough, symptoms will occur. Decompression sickness may be defined as a condition where gaseous bubbles are formed due to pressure gradients between the environment and tissues with accompanying symptoms corresponding to bubble location.

Bubble Formation and Development

Bubbles are formed for a variety of reasons; the most direct effect is associated with rate of ascent. The bubbles start as a vapor phase (gas nucleolus) and may attain critical size or more, thus producing symptoms. It is believed that on most dives bubbles may form but not exceed critical size. Such bubbles are usually referred to as "silent bubbles" and do not produce immediate symptoms.

It is understood that pressure change, exposure time, gas solubility, gas diffusion or perfusion, tissue vascularity, and biophysical processes of bubble formation all contribute to the formation of bubbles. When viewed from a practical standpoint bubble formation raises several other questions, such as the role of exercise, blood changes, possible role of carbon dioxide, and body composition.

The role of exercise in the production of decompression sickness has often been debated. Early investigators believed that exercise during decompression promoted good circulation and should be recommended. Recently the role of exercise has been looked at more closely. When a diver performs exercise, such as moving an arm or doing kneebends, he may experience bubble formation due to movement of supersaturated liquid (tissues). Motion causes low-pressure regions to be created, and gas attempting to pass through a restriction such as an artery constricted due to exercise will produce bubbles. The rapid motion in exercise can produce cavities, which are quickly filled with gases, and bubbles may be formed. Experiments have shown that animals and men decompressed on marginal schedules that should not produce symptoms, do in fact produce symptoms in a limb that is exercised during decompression; unexercised limbs do not develop symptoms. Other reasons exercise produces bubbles are greater gas uptake, increased carbon dioxide production, and general circulatory effects. Exercise should be limited as much as possible during a dive, and should be avoided during decompression and immediately after surfacing.

During decompression there is plasma loss, and agglutination of erythrocytes occurs. (Formed elements of blood lose their common repulsion, tend to agglomerate and adhere to vessel walls, and embolization may occur). Lipemia, which influences gas solubility and saturation of the blood, occurs after large meals. Fatty foods increase the susceptibility to bends because of the increased blood lipids (and cholesterol, and triglycerides). Alcohol also causes an increase in blood lipids; drinking alcoholic beverages within 6 to 12 hours prior to diving increases the susceptibility to bends. Even smoking induces a temporary increase in blood lipids.

In the event of dehydration, fluid balance changes result in changes in the ratio of fat to water in the body. The less fluid, the higher the fat to blood ratio. Loss of body fluid is related to blood and interstitial volume, and thus interferes with gas transports during decompression.

The role of carbon dioxide in the development of gas bubbles and their growth cannot be overemphasized. Carbon dioxide is 50 times more soluble in fat than nitrogen; thus it is a contributor to the development of decompression sickness. The more carbon dioxide produced, the greater the probability of bends.

Obviously anything that interferes with or restricts circulation or respiration is an additive factor to bubble formation. Tourniquets or overly tight wet suits that restrict blood vessels may result in bubble formation. Smoking and alcohol intake both affect the respiratory and circulatory systems, thus increasing the susceptibility to bends. Respiratory disorders such as colds interfere with effective gas exchange and should be deterrents to diving.

Body composition is also a major contributor to developing decompression sickness. Many investigators feel that the ratio of fat to total body weight is the most important consideration in determining an individual's susceptibility to bends. Nitrogen is five times as soluble in fat as in aqueous tissue. As early as 1878 Paul Bert observed that lean animals were not as susceptible to bends as fat ones. Further experiments have revealed that most bubbles observed are in fatty tissues or veins draining fatty areas. Fat holds more nitrogen after decompression and increases the possibility of decompression sickness when the diver is performing repetitive dives. The fact that the higher the fat content the greater the bends susceptibility has been well documented by Behnke, Boycott, Damant, Philp, and many others.

Perhaps a good experiment to illustrate the effect of fat on decompression was one performed by Philp (1967). This experiment consisted of taking 55 white male rats, born on the same day, and feeding them the same foods except for total calories. The rats were kept on the same exercise routine. The rats were divided into five groups according to body weight. After six weeks they were compressed to 112 feet for 2 hours, then safely decompressed to the surface (5 minutes at 56 feet, 5 minutes at 28 feet, and 5 minutes at 14 feet, a total decompression of 17 minutes). The rats were then decompressed to an altitude of 10,000 feet while performing moderate exercise. The results are in Table 5.

Table 5. Effect of Fat on Decompression in Rats

Group	Av. wt. (gm.)	Fat to body wt. (%)	Incidence of decompression sickness (%)			
			None	Mild	Serious	Death
A	171.3	1.92	100			
B	286.6	5.18	36	64		
C	331.4	8.42		63	37	
D	364.5	10.76	9	45	37	9
E	379.6	15.11		64	27	9

Bubbles occur both within and out of the circulation (intravascular-extravascular) and may result in hypoxia, necrosis, compression of nerves, vascular irritants, and pulmonary edema.

Preventing symptoms from bubble formation depends upon consideration of all contributing factors (see Figure 21).

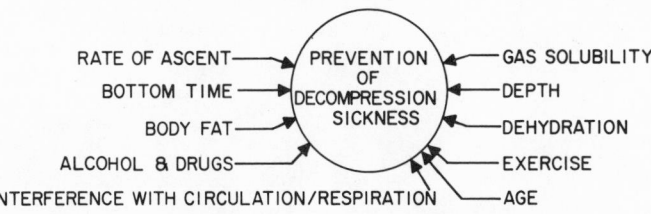

Fig. 21. Contributing factors to decompression sickness.

Another major contributor to decompression sickness is temperature. A cold diver is much more susceptible to bends than a warm diver. A diver should take the following protective steps to avoid decompression sickness.

Maintain body heat
Eat a high protein diet, especially during diving operations
Avoid alcohol within 6 to 12 hours of a dive
Avoid smoking within one hour before or after a dive

Keep body fat to a minimum
Select properly fitted wet suits
Avoid exercise during decompression
Increase fluid intake during diving operations
Avoid diving with colds or respiratory infections

Older divers should place greater emphasis on avoiding contributory factors to bubble formation.

Organ and System Involvement

As mentioned earlier, the exact symptoms of decompression sickness will depend upon bubble location. Generally speaking, almost all organs and systems of the body are subject to symptoms. Neurological decompression sickness is the most severe form and is present in a relatively low percentage of the total cases reported. Joint involvement is the most common, and bone changes represent a form of delayed decompression sickness.

Neurological decompression sickness can be subdivided into that of the central nervous system (brain and spinal cord), which results in symptoms of paralysis, dizziness, loss of bowel or bladder control, unconsciousness, blurry vision, convulsion, and pins-and-needles sensations; and that of the peripheral nervous system (cranial and spinal nerves), which has symptoms of numbness, cool and woolly feet, and weakness.

Neurological decompression sickness is frequently hard to treat and usually is the result of major errors in decompression technique. Careful consideration should be given to patients with neurological decompression sickness before returning them to active diving status. Neurological decompression sickness is often referred to as staggers.

Joint involvement, known more commonly as the bends, is the most common symptom. In divers it is more common in the upper extremities. It is characterized by pain and swelling and usually responds well to treatment.

Decompression sickness of the respiratory system, often called chokes, can be quite serious. Symptoms consist of a burning sensation in the chest, a choking feeling, shallow breathing, coughing, loss of consciousness, and shock.

Skin bends result when bubbles occur at the skin and is characterized by a red rash and itching. When not associated with other symptoms, it is not considered to be serious.

Unusual fatigue is also felt to be a symptom of decompression sickness, and some physiologists feel it is associated with early symptoms of a neurological decompression sickness.

Bone changes or aseptic bone necrosis represent a delayed form of decompression sickness. Symptoms of this disease take three months to five years before developing, and frequently this disease cripples the afflicted diver. Many physiologists believe that aseptic bone necrosis is caused by gas bubbles forming in the nutrient arteries supplying the bone. These bubbles cut off circulation to the bone, and as a result the bone cells die. When this happens in the shaft of the bone, no problem arises because eventually new blood vessels supply the area and new calcium is laid down. New calcium is not laid down smoothly but in a random manner referred to as creeping substitution. These lesions when found in the shaft are symptomless and of no consequence. If, however, these lesions occur at the head of the bone, such as the shoulder or hip, major problems arise. Due to constant usage and the forces exerted on these joints in normal work, the joints begin to fragment and chip. The fragmented chips cause more abrasion, and eventually the entire joint is ground up. Other physiologists believe that this disease is caused by the rate of compression. Additional research in the cause and prevention of aseptic bone necrosis is needed.

The body areas most normally involved are shoulders, hips, and knees, with most cases occurring in the shoulders and hips. Unfortunately, a single exposure to depths below 38 feet has been documented as the cause of this problem in a group of men, even though they exhibited no other symptoms of decompression sickness. Divers who occasionally short themselves on decompression, by coming up too soon or by averaging depths instead of decompressing for the greatest depth and bottom time, those who perform routine extreme exposure dives, and saturation divers are more prone to developing this disease. It can occur without ever experiencing other symptoms of decompression sickness. Faulty treatment is also believed to be a major contributor to this disease.

Aseptic bone necrosis is detectable in early stages only through X-rays. By the time symptoms occur, the diver is too far along for a total cure, although corrective surgery may accomplish limited improvement.

Aseptic bone necrosis is a threat to all divers who do not follow recognized decompression tables correctly. Even when these tables are followed correctly there is a marginal risk of developing this disease, so again it should be emphasized that the tables should be followed accurately and possibly conservatively. The extra time taken for decompression today may result in walking five years from now. Some very conservative divers advocate decompression on the next greater schedule, either per the next longer bottom time or according to a schedule 10 feet deeper than the dive performed. There are many divers who "logic" out dives. For example, "the bottom time was 40 minutes with a maximum depth of 180 feet; 30 minutes of this time were spent at 140 feet so the average depth is 160; and the decompression schedule used is 160 feet for 40 minutes." Frequently these divers surface with no symptoms of decompression sickness, but perhaps their X-rays will prove interesting in a few years. It is wiser to be safe and take the extra decompression time and therefore avoid increased risk of decompression sickness now or five years from now.

The diver should not only know the symptoms of decompression sickness but should also know to which system each symptom is related. Most neurological symptoms will occur within one hour of surfacing. Approximately 85% of the symptoms of decompression sickness will occur within 1 hour, and only 1% develop after 6 hours. There are, however, documented cases occurring as late as 48 hours following a dive. These figures, of course, do not include aseptic bone necrosis. The latter is avoidable through either avoiding decompression dives or by performing conservative decompressions.

Prevention of Decompression Sickness

Development of a safe ascent rate is the secret to preventing symptoms of decompression sickness. Professor Haldane, considered the father of modern decompression technique, based his theory of a safe ascent rate (decompression) on three assumptions:

1. Prediction of degree of saturation of tissues and blood after a given time at a specific depth.

2. Determination of the amount of supersaturation that can be tolerated without symptoms.

3. Incorporating, in the water, stops at the point where the critical threshold of supersaturation is reached (staged decompression).

In the first assumption, consideration had to be given to the different tissues and their solubility to nitrogen and to the establishment of a time relationship for these tissues becoming saturated. To do this Haldane incorporated the use of tissue half-times, which represent the time it takes a particular tissue to become 50% saturated at a specific depth. This development yielded the present-day term of bottom time, which is a statement based on measurements of the degree of saturation in the body at a given depth for a particular time (actually starting from time descent is first begun until ascent commences). In establishing this concept it was found that tissues take up gas rapidly at first but more slowly as a state of equilibrium is reached. Also, some tissues were discovered to react quickly to increased depths (fast tissues) and others to respond slowly (slow tissues).

In Figure 22 a graph represents a theoretical tissue saturation curve. The values in this curve are not perfectly accurate but suffice for explanation.

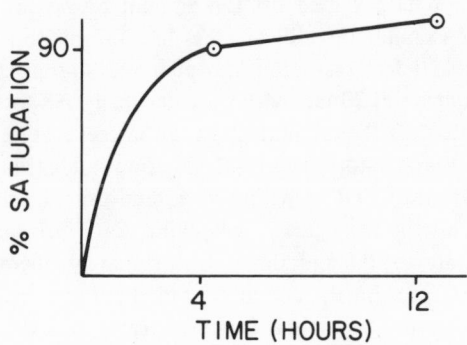

Fig. 22. Theoretical tissue saturation curve.

Once the degree of saturation has been determined, the next step is to compute a safe ascent rate. Before this rate could be established, however, the degree of supersaturation that can be tolerated without an individual developing symptoms had to be determined (supersaturation means excessive pressure). A mathematical model was devised using m values. These m values were originally set up to represent a tissue ratio of 2 to 1 (it was believed the tissues could contain 2 times as much pressure as the environmental pressure without developing symptoms). In the field, however, this ratio proved to be unacceptable and has been revised to 1:58 to 1.

From this ratio it was determined that a linear ascent rate of 60 feet per minute was acceptable until the bottom time exceeds certain limitations. With longer bottom times the tissues become saturated to a point that they reach critical supersaturation prior to surfacing. To compensate for this effect it was necessary to incorporate stops (staged decompression) at different depths in the water. When performing decompression dives, the diver comes up to the point of critical supersaturation and then stops until the degree of supersaturation has dropped sufficiently to allow him to ascend further to another stop or to the surface. It is important for the diver to realize that the stop is at the point of critical supersaturation and that further ascent will most likely produce symptoms.

Stops represent a theoretical barrier that should not be broken. The time of a stop is planned on the assumption of venting off gas (decompressing) from the tissue at the maximum rate due to the 1:58 to 1 tissue versus environment ratio. A stop below the specified depth will yield a different tissue versus environment ratio and result in slower tissue decompression than calculated. Therefore, when the diver ascends to the next stop he may not have vented off the amount of gas pressure that was calculated. For example: If a diver takes his 30-foot stop at 35 feet and then ascends to 20 feet (assuming he spent the 30-foot stop time at 35 feet) he would arrive at 20 feet with a greater than 1:58 to 1 ratio because he had not vented off the amount of gas at 35 feet that he would have at the scheduled 30-foot stop. The same situation holds true for extending time of stops arbitrarily (if he wishes to extend time, he should do so by decompressing on the next greater schedule). A perfect decompression is based on accurate depths and times. Unfortunately, there are few truly accurate depth gauges on the commercial market today. Some divers take stops two feet deeper than their gauge indicates, unless they know the exact calibration of their depth gauge.

Many divers fail to realize that the final staged stop is at the surface. On a dive within 10 minutes of a decompression dive or on a decompression dive, the surface should be treated with the same respect as any other decompression stop. Exercise should be avoided (hauling up the anchor line, stowing tanks, performing strenuous labor) for a reasonable period of time. A rule of thumb is complete rest for 10 minutes and only moderate exercise for at least the same time duration as the 10-foot stop.

Flying is another method of pressure reduction and should be avoided immediately after diving. On dives that are not within 10 minutes of a decompression dive, a surface interval of at least 4 hours should exist prior to flying. On dives involving decompression it is our opinion that a surface interval of 24 hours should occur before flying. Many divers, however, fly after attaining repetitive group C or after 6 hours. Still, for maximum safety it is best to spend 12 to 24 hours on the surface before flying.

When diving at altitudes higher than sea level, the tables must be modified. Currently, the only modification available is the table by E. R. Cross shown at the end of this chapter along with standard dive tables. Prevention of decompression sickness is achieved by following the dive tables accurately and avoiding conditions that contribute to the development of symptoms.

First Aid and Treatment of Decompression Sickness

When following dive tables accurately, we can anticipate a 5% incidence of decompression sickness due to individual susceptibility and errors in decompression technique. Proper first aid and treatment are necessary to avoid the risk of permanent injury from decompression sickness.

First aid is simple and involves general first aid practice (observe for shock, resuscitate if necessary). The diver should not be given drugs or pain relievers (unless by a doctor), and if possible he should be kept at rest and breathing oxygen. When oxygen is administered, care should be taken to remove all oil from the victim's body, especially his mouth (chapstick, suntan oil, etc.). The U.S. Coast Guard or emergency rescue service should be contacted (inland, the highway patrol), and arrangements made to get the victim to the nearest chamber. Each diver should be aware of the location of decompression chambers in the area where he is diving.

At the treatment facility the patient will most likely be treated using one of two oxygen treatment tables. The diver is usually compressed to a depth of 60 feet and administered pur oxygen with air breaks in between. These tables range in duration from 135 to 285 minutes. If the symptoms are severe enough or if air embolism is suspected, the diver may be compressed to 165 feet, in which case the tables would range from 154 minutes to 319 minutes. The use of oxygen tables is approximately 85% effective.

A diver exhibiting symptoms of simple bends (bends occurring after surfacing and joint pain only) will be treated according to the 135-minute table. Divers with neurological symptoms or respiratory symptoms on bends occurring in the water will be treated on the 285-minute schedule. Air embolism cases will be treated on one of the 165-foot tables, 154 to 319 minutes. A diver who does not experience relief will be switched to the next greater table. Divers who have recurrences during treatment will also be switched to the next greater table.

When neurological decompression sickness is treated, dextran and steroids may be administered while the patient is still in the chamber. If the patient does not respond initially to treatment he may be treated again 4 to 12 hours after the first treatment run. Patients who do not respond initially to treatment often have been found to respond to a sequence of 30-foot oxygen-breathing periods over several days, especially when this treatment is combined with dextran. Frequently tables will be modified by the medical consultant or with his permission by the chamber attendant during any given treatment run. In some cases plasma may also be given to the patient.

Special consideration must be given to ensure that the patient is free of oil on his body and that all fire hazards are removed from the patient, tender, and chamber. The chamber must be ventilated at regular intervals to avoid carbon dioxide buildup or high oxygen concentrations. Compression is usually made at 25 feet per minute or as fast as the victim can be compressed. In compression the temperature in the chamber is increased and the chamber may be noisy, and on ascent the chamber will cool down and may become "foggy." It is important that the patient be aware of these occurrences in order to avoid undue anxiety or stress that may interfere with treatment. It is also important that the patient be medically examined at depth and each time he is decompressed to a different depth. No sleeping is allowed during changes in depth or oxygen-breathing periods. During air breaks the patient should be administered fluids to prevent further dehydration. Body position is important in that the patient should not sit or lie in a position that will interfere with good circulation. After treatment the patient should be placed under medical observation. A minimum dry period of two weeks should exist before diving is resumed, and the diver should undergo a thorough physical examination at that time.

Interrupted Decompression Procedures

In the event a diver surfaces during decompression, there are two procedures from which he may choose to complete his decompression. The first of these is our preferred method because of its simplicity.

Within 5 minutes descend to a depth 30 feet deeper than the original, first-scheduled stop. At the new depth remain 5 minutes, add 10 minutes to the original bottom time, and complete decompression on this schedule. For example: a diver attains a depth of 100 feet with a bottom time of 30 minutes. During ascent he accidently surfaces. His original schedule required a stop at 10 feet for 3 minutes [per Table 6 (U.S. Navy Table 1-10)]. To utilize the emergency schedule he must descend to 40 feet for 5 minutes, then add 10 minutes to his original bottom time. Thus, he will complete decompression as if the dive had been 100 feet for 40 minutes. According to Table 6 this would be 15 minutes at 10 feet.

The second method is to return to the water within 3.5 minutes, descend to 40 feet, and then to remain at 40 feet for one-fourth of the schedule 10-foot stop time, ascend to 30 feet for one-third of the 10-foot stop time, to 20 feet for one-half of the 10-foot stop time, and finally to 10 feet for one and one-half the 10-foot stop time. For example: a diver accidentally surfaces from a dive to 100 feet for 40 minutes. Within 3.5

minutes he enters the water and then decompresses as follows (his original stop should have been 15 minutes at 10 feet): 3.75 or 4 minutes at 40 feet, 5 minutes at 30 feet, 7.5 or 8 minutes at 20 feet, and 22.5 or 23 minutes at 10 feet.

In summary, although decompression sickness is a very real possibility like all other diving maladies it can be avoided through following accepted decompression models, employing good decompression technique, and maintaining good physical conditioning.

It should be obvious that drinking alcohol within 6 hours of a dive or smoking immediately prior to or following a decompression dive will increase the probability of decompression sickness.

Divers should eat at intervals that keep the blood sugar level normal and concentrate on foods that are low in fat content. Special care should be taken to ensure that protective clothing is not too tight, and exercise should be kept as light as possible.

Divers should use an accurate depth gauge and avoid exerting and bouncing up and down during decompression. Stops should be timed accurately and respiration kept normal. While performing the dive, the diver should try to maintain good body positioning, as this will result in less drag and therefore reduce the work load and carbon dioxide production.

Decompression Procedures

General Instructions for Air Diving

Need for Decompression

A quantity of nitrogen is taken up by the body during every dive. The amount absorbed depends upon the depth of the dive and the exposure (bottom) time. If the quantity of nitrogen dissolved in the body tissues exceeds a certain critical amount, the ascent must be delayed to allow the body tissue to remove the excess nitrogen. Decompression sickness results from failure to delay the ascent and to allow this process of gradual desaturation. A specified time at a specific depth for purposes of desaturation is called a decompression stop.

No-Decompression Schedules

Dives that are not long or deep enough to require decompression stops are no-decompression dives. Dives to 33 feet or less do not require decompression stops. As the depth increases, the allowable bottom time for no-decompression dives decreases. Five minutes at 190 feet is the deepest no-decompression schedule. These dives are all listed in the No-Decompression Limits and Repetitive Group Designation Table for No-Decompression Dives (No-Decompression Table [Table 8]), and only require compliance with the 60-feet-per-minute rate of ascent.

Schedules That Require Decompression Stops

All dives beyond the limits of the No-Decompression Table require decompression stops. These dives are listed in the U.S. Navy Standard Air Decompression Table (Table 6). Comply exactly with instructions except as modified by surface decompression procedures.

Variations in Rate of Ascent

Ascend from all dives at the rate of 60 feet per minute.

In the event you are unable to maintain the 60-feet-per-minute rate of ascent:

(*a*) If the delay was at a depth greater than 50 feet: increase the bottom time by the difference between the time used in ascent and the time that should have been used at a rate of 60 feet per minute. Decompress according to the requirements of the new total bottom time.

(*b*) If the delay was at a depth less than 50 feet: increase the first stop by the difference between the time used in ascent and the time that should have been used at the rate of 60 feet per minute.

Repetitive Dive Procedure

A dive performed within 12 hours of surfacing from a previous dive is a repetitive dive. The period between dives is the surface interval. Excess nitrogen requires 12 hours to be effectively lost from the body. These tables are designed to protect the diver from the effects of this residual nitrogen. Allow a minimum surface interval of 10 minutes between all dives. For any interval under 10 minutes, add the bottom time of the previous dives to that of the repetitive dive and choose the decompression schedule for the total bottom time and the deepest dive. Specific instructions are given for the use of each table in the following order:

(1) The No-Decompression Table or the U.S. Navy Standard Air Decompression Table gives the repetitive group designation for all schedules which may precede a repetitive dive.

(2) The Surface Interval Credit Table gives credit for the desaturation occurring during the surface interval.

(3) The Repetitive Dive Timetable gives the number of minutes of residual nitrogen time to add to the actual bottom time of the repetitive dive to obtain decompression for the residual nitrogen.

(4) The No-Decompression Table of the U.S. Navy Standard Air Decompression Table gives the decompression required for the repetitive dive.

U.S. Navy Standard Air Decompression Table

Instructions for Use

Time of decompression stops in the table is in minutes.

Enter the table at the exact or the next greater depth than the maximum depth attained during the dive. Select the listed bottom time that is exactly equal to or is next greater than the bottom time of the dive. Maintain the diver's chest as close as possible to each decompression depth for the number of minutes listed. The rate of ascent *between* stops is not critical for stops of 50 feet or less. Commence timing each stop on arrival at the decompression depth and resume ascent when the specified time has lapsed.

For example—a dive to 82 feet for 36 minutes. To determine the proper decompression procedure: The next greater depth listed in this table is 90 feet. The next greater bottom time listed opposite 90 feet is 40. Stop 7 minutes at 10 feet in accordance with the 90/40 schedule.

For example—a dive to 110 feet for 30 minutes. It is known that the depth did not exceed 110 feet. To determine the proper decompression schedule: The exact depth of 110 feet is listed. The exact bottom time of 30 minutes is listed opposite 110 feet. Decompress according to the 110/30 schedule unless the dive was particularly cold or arduous. In that case, go to the schedule for the next deeper and longer dive, i.e., 120/40.

Table 6. U.S. Navy Standard Air Decompression Table

Depth (feet)	Bottom time (min)	Time to first stop (min:sec)	Decompression stops (feet) 50	40	30	20	10	Total ascent (min:sec)	Repetitive group
40	200	----------					0	0:40	(*)
	210	0:30					2	2:40	N
	230	0:30					7	7:40	N
	250	0:30					11	11:40	O
	270	0:30					15	15:40	O
	300	0:30					19	19:40	Z
50	100	----------					0	0:50	(*)
	110	0:40					3	3:50	L
	120	0:40					5	5:50	M
	140	0:40					10	10:50	M
	160	0:40					21	21:50	N
	180	0:40					29	29:50	O
	200	0:40					35	35:50	O
	220	0:40					40	40:50	Z
	240	0:40					47	47:50	Z
60	60	----------					0	1:00	(*)
	70	0:50					2	3:00	K
	80	0:50					7	8:00	L
	100	0:50					14	15:00	M
	120	0:50					26	27:00	N
	140	0:50					39	40:00	O
	160	0:50					48	49:00	Z
	180	0:50					56	57:00	Z
	200	0:40					1	69	71:00	Z
70	50	----------					0	1:10	(*)
	60	1:00					8	9:10	K
	70	1:00					14	15:10	L
	80	1:00					18	19:10	M
	90	1:00					23	24:10	N
	100	1:00					33	34:10	N
	110	0:50					2	41	44:10	O
	120	0:50					4	47	52:10	O
	130	0:50					6	52	59:10	O
	140	0:50					8	56	65:10	Z
	150	0:50					9	61	71:10	Z
	160	0:50					13	72	86:10	Z
	170	0:50					19	79	99:10	Z
80	40	----------					0	1:20	(*)
	50	1:10					10	11:20	K
	60	1:10					17	18:20	L
	70	1:10					23	24:20	M
	80	1:00					2	31	34:20	N
	90	1:00					7	39	47:20	N
	100	1:00					11	46	58:20	O
	110	1:00					13	53	67:20	O
	120	1:00					17	56	74:20	Z
	130	1:00					19	63	83:20	Z
	140	1:00					26	69	96:20	Z
	150	1:00					32	77	110:20	Z
90	30	----------					0	1:30	(*)
	40	1:20					7	8:30	J
	50	1:20					18	19:30	L
	60	1:20					25	26:30	M
	70	1:10					7	30	38:30	N
	80	1:10					13	40	54:30	N
	90	1:10					18	48	67:30	O
	100	1:10					21	54	76:30	Z
	110	1:10					24	61	86:30	Z
	120	1:10					32	68	101:30	Z
	130	1:00			5		36	74	116:30	Z

Table 6. U.S. Navy Standard Air Decompression Table (cont'd.)

Depth (feet)	Bottom time (min)	Time to first stop (min:sec)	Decompression stops (feet) 50	40	30	20	10	Total ascent (min:sec)	Repetitive group
100—Continued	25	--------	--------	--------	--------	--------		0	1:40	(*)
	30	1:30	--------	--------	--------	--------		3	4:40	I
	40	1:30	--------	--------	--------	--------		15	16:40	K
	50	1:20	--------	--------	--------		2	24	27:40	L
	60	1:20	--------	--------	--------		9	28	38:40	N
	70	1:20	--------	--------	--------		17	39	57:40	O
	80	1:20	--------	--------	--------		23	48	72:40	O
	90	1:10	--------	--------	3	23	57	84:40	Z
	100	1:10	--------	--------	7	23	66	97:40	Z
	110	1:10	--------	--------	10	34	72	117:40	Z
	120	1:10	--------	--------	12	41	78	132:40	Z
110	20	--------	--------	--------	--------	--------		0	1:50	(*)
	25	1:40	--------	--------	--------	--------		3	4:50	H
	30	1:40	--------	--------	--------	--------		7	8:50	J
	40	1:30	--------	--------	--------		2	21	24:50	L
	50	1:30	--------	--------	--------		8	26	35:50	M
	60	1:30	--------	--------	--------		18	36	55:50	N
	70	1:20	--------	--------	1	23	48	73:50	O
	80	1:20	--------	--------	7	23	57	88:50	Z
	90	1:20	--------	--------	12	30	64	107:50	Z
	100	1:20	--------	--------	15	37	72	125:50	Z
120	15	--------	--------	--------	--------	--------		0	2:00	(*)
	20	1:50	--------	--------	--------	--------		2	4:00	H
	25	1:50	--------	--------	--------	--------		6	8:00	I
	30	1:50	--------	--------	--------	--------		14	16:00	J
	40	1:40	--------	--------	--------		5	25	32:00	L
	50	1:40	--------	--------	--------		15	31	48:00	N
	60	1:30	--------	--------	2	22	45	71:00	O
	70	1:30	--------	--------	9	23	55	89:00	O
	80	1:30	--------	--------	15	27	63	107:00	Z
	90	1:30	--------	--------	19	37	74	132:00	Z
	100	1:30	--------	--------	23	45	80	150:00	Z
130	10	--------	--------	--------	--------	--------		0	2:10	(*)
	15	2:00	--------	--------	--------	--------		1	3:10	F
	20	2:00	--------	--------	--------	--------		4	6:10	H
	25	2:00	--------	--------	--------	--------		10	12:10	J
	30	1:50	--------	--------	--------	3	18	23:10	M
	40	1:50	--------	--------	--------	10	25	37:10	N
	50	1:40	--------	--------	3	21	37	63:10	O
	60	1:40	--------	--------	9	23	52	86:10	Z
	70	1:40	--------	--------	16	24	61	103:10	Z
	80	1:30	--------	3	19	35	72	131:10	Z
	90	1:30	--------	8	19	45	80	154:10	Z
140	10	--------	--------	--------	--------	--------		0	2:20	(*)
	15	2:10	--------	--------	--------	--------		2	4:20	G
	20	2:10	--------	--------	--------	--------		6	8:20	I
	25	2:00	--------	--------	--------		2	14	18:20	J
	30	2:00	--------	--------	--------		5	21	28:20	K
	40	1:50	--------	--------	2	16	26	46:20	N
	50	1:50	--------	--------	6	24	44	76:20	O
	60	1:50	--------	--------	16	23	56	97:20	Z
	70	1:40	--------	4	19	32	68	125:20	Z
	80	1:40	--------	10	23	41	79	155:20	Z
150	5	--------	--------	--------	--------	--------		0	2:30	C
	10	2:20	--------	--------	--------	--------		1	3:30	E
	15	2:20	--------	--------	--------	--------		3	5:30	G
	20	2:10	--------	--------	--------		2	7	11:30	H
	25	2:10	--------	--------	--------		4	17	23:30	K
	30	2:10	--------	--------	--------		8	24	34:30	L
	40	2:00	--------	--------	5	19	33	59:30	N
	50	2:00	--------	--------	12	23	51	88:30	O

Table 6. U.S. Navy Standard Air Decompression Table (cont'd.)

Depth (feet)	Bottom time (min)	Time to first stop (min:sec)	Decompression stops (feet)					Total ascent (min:sec)	Repetitive group
			50	40	30	20	10		
150—Continued	60	1:50		3	19	26	62	112:30	Z
	70	1:50		11	19	39	75	146:30	Z
	80	1:40	1	17	19	50	84	173:30	Z
160	5						0	2:40	D
	10	2:30					1	3:40	F
	15	2:20				1	4	7:40	H
	20	2:20				3	11	16:40	J
	25	2:20				7	20	29:40	K
	30	2:10			2	11	25	40:40	M
	40	2:10			7	23	39	71:40	N
	50	2:00		2	16	23	55	98:40	Z
	60	2:00		9	19	33	69	132:40	Z
	70	1:50	1	17	22	44	80	166:40	Z
170	5						0	2:50	D
	10	2:40					2	4:50	F
	15	2:30				2	5	9:50	H
	20	2:30				4	15	21:50	J
	25	2:20			2	7	23	34:50	L
	30	2:20			4	13	26	45:50	M
	40	2:10		1	10	23	45	81:50	O
	50	2:10		5	18	23	61	109:50	Z
	60	2:00	2	15	22	37	74	152:50	Z
	70	2:00	8	17	19	51	86	183:50	Z
180	5						0	3:00	D
	10	2:50					3	6:00	F
	15	2:40				3	6	12:00	I
	20	2:30			1	5	17	26:00	K
	25	2:30			3	10	24	40:00	L
	30	2:30			6	17	27	53:00	N
	40	2:20		3	14	23	50	93:00	O
	50	2:10	2	9	19	30	65	128:00	Z
	60	2:10	5	16	19	44	81	168:00	Z
190	5						0	3:10	D
	10	2:50				1	3	7:10	G
	15	2:50				4	7	14:10	I
	20	2:40			2	6	20	31:10	K
	25	2:40			5	11	25	44:10	M
	30	2:30		1	8	19	32	63:10	N
	40	2:30		8	14	23	55	103:10	O
	50	2:20	4	13	22	33	72	147:10	Z
	60	2:20	10	17	19	50	84	183:10	Z

*See table 1–11 for repetitive groups in no-decompression dives.

From Table 1-10, 1970 *U.S. Navy Diving Manual.*

Table 7. Experimental Repetitive Dive Table for Extreme Exposures

Depth (ft)	Bottom time (min)	Time to first stop (min:sec)	Decompression stops (feet)													Total ascent time (min:sec)	Repetitive group
			130	120	110	100	90	80	70	60	50	40	30	20	10		
200	5	3:10													1	4:20	E
	10	3:00												1	4	8:20	G
	15	2:50											1	4	10	18:20	J
	20	2:50											3	7	27	40:20	L
	25	2:50											7	14	25	49:20	M
	30	2:40										2	9	22	37	73:20	O
	40	2:30									2	8	17	23	59	112:20	Z
	50	2:30									6	16	22	39	75	161:20	Z
	60	2:20								2	13	17	24	51	89	199:20	Z
	90	1:50					1	10	10	12	12	30	38	74	134	324:20	Z
	120	1:40				6	10	10	10	24	28	40	64	98	180	473:20	Z
	180	1:20		1	10	10	18	24	24	42	48	70	106	142	187	685:20	Z
	240	1:20		6	20	24	24	36	42	54	68	114	122	142	187	842:20	Z
	360	1:10	12	22	36	40	44	56	82	98	100	114	122	142	187	1058:20	Z
210	5	3:20													1	4:30	E
	10	3:10												2	4	9:30	G
	15	3:00											1	5	13	22:30	J
	20	3:00											4	10	23	40:30	L
	25	2:50										2	7	17	27	56:30	N
	30	2:50										4	9	24	41	81:30	O
	40	2:40									4	9	19	26	63	124:30	Z
	50	2:30								1	9	17	19	45	80	174:30	Z
220	5	3:30													2	5:40	E
	10	3:20												2	5	10:40	H
	15	3:10											2	5	16	26:40	J
	20	3:00										1	3	11	24	42:40	L
	25	3:00										3	8	19	33	66:40	N
	30	2:50									1	7	10	23	47	91:40	O
	40	2:50									6	12	22	29	68	140:40	Z
	50	2:40								3	12	17	18	51	86	190:40	Z
230	5	3:40													2	5:50	E
	10	3:20											1	2	6	12:50	H
	15	3:20											3	6	18	30:50	K
	20	3:10										2	5	12	26	48:50	M
	25	3:10										4	8	22	37	74:50	O
	30	3:00									2	8	12	23	51	99:50	O
	40	2:50								1	7	15	22	34	74	156:50	Z
	50	2:50								5	14	16	24	51	89	202:50	Z
240	5	3:50													2	6:00	E
	10	3:30											1	3	6	14:00	I
	15	3:30											4	6	21	35:00	K
	20	3:20										3	6	15	25	53:00	M
	25	3:10									1	4	9	24	40	82:00	O
	30	3:10									4	8	15	22	56	109:00	O
	40	3:00								3	7	17	22	39	75	167:00	Z
	50	2:50							1	8	15	16	29	51	94	218:00	Z
250	5	3:50												1	2	7:10	F
	10	3:40											1	4	7	16:10	I
	15	3:30										1	4	7	22	38:10	K
	20	3:30										4	7	17	27	59:10	N
	25	3:20									2	7	10	24	45	92:10	O
	30	3:20									6	7	17	23	59	116:10	Z
	40	3:10								5	9	17	19	45	79	178:10	Z
	60	2:40					4	10	10	10	12	22	36	64	126	298:10	Z
	90	2:10		8	10	10	10	10	10	28	28	44	68	98	186	514:10	Z
260	5	4:00												1	2	7:20	F
	10	3:50											2	4	9	19:20	J
	15	3:40										2	4	10	22	42:20	L
	20	3:30									1	4	7	20	31	67:20	N
	25	3:30									3	8	11	23	50	99:20	O
	30	3:20								2	6	8	19	26	61	126:20	Z
	40	3:10							1	6	11	16	19	49	84	190:20	Z
270	5	4:10												1	3	8:30	F
	10	4:00											2	5	11	22:30	I
	15	3:50										3	4	11	24	46:30	L
	20	3:40									2	3	9	21	35	74:30	O

Table 7. Experimental Repetitive Dive Table for Extreme Exposures (cont'd.)

Depth (ft)	Bottom time (min)	Time to first stop (min:sec)	Decompression stops (feet) 130	120	110	100	90	80	70	60	50	40	30	20	10	Total ascent time (min:sec)	Repetitive group
270—Con.	25	3:30								2	3	8	13	23	53	106:30	O
	30	3:30								3	6	12	22	27	64	138:30	Z
	40	3:20							5	6	11	17	22	51	88	204:30	Z
280	5	4:20												2	2	8:40	F
	10	4:00										1	2	5	13	25:40	J
	15	3:50									1	3	4	11	26	49:40	M
	20	3:50									3	4	8	23	39	81:40	O
	25	3:40								2	5	7	16	23	56	113:40	Z
	30	3:30							1	3	7	13	22	30	70	150:40	Z
	40	3:20						1	6	6	13	17	27	51	93	218:40	Z
290	5	4:30												2	3	9:50	F
	10	4:10										1	3	5	16	29:50	J
	15	4:00									1	3	6	12	26	52:50	M
	20	4:00									3	7	9	23	43	89:50	O
	25	3:50								3	5	8	17	23	60	120:50	Z
	30	3:40							1	5	6	16	22	36	72	162:50	Z
	40	3:30						3	5	7	15	16	32	51	95	228:50	Z
300	5	4:40												3	3	11:00	G
	10	4:20										1	3	6	17	32:00	K
	15	4:10									2	3	6	15	26	57:00	M
	20	4:00								2	3	7	10	23	47	97:00	O
	25	3:50							1	3	6	8	19	26	61	129:00	Z
	30	3:50							2	5	7	17	22	39	75	172:00	Z
	40	3:40						4	6	9	15	17	34	51	90	231:00	Z
	60	3:00		4	10	10	10	10	10	14	28	32	50	90	187	460:00	Z

From the U.S. Navy Standard Air Decompression Table for Exceptional Exposures. The repetitive groups were calculated by Aubrey Melton III.

Table 8. No Decompression Limits and Repetitive Group Designation Table for No-Decompression Air Dives

Depth (feet)	No-decom-pression limits (min)	Repetitive groups (air dives)														
		A	B	C	D	E	F	G	H	I	J	K	L	M	N	O
10	----------	60	120	210	300											
15	----------	35	70	110	160	225	350									
20	----------	25	50	75	100	135	180	240	325							
25	----------	20	35	55	75	100	125	160	195	245	315					
30	----------	15	30	45	60	75	95	120	145	170	205	250	310			
35	310	5	15	25	40	50	60	80	100	120	140	160	190	220	270	310
40	200	5	15	25	30	40	50	70	80	100	110	130	150	170	200	
50	100		10	15	25	30	40	50	60	70	80	90	100			
60	60		10	15	20	25	30	40	50	55	60					
70	50		5	10	15	20	30	35	40	45	50					
80	40		5	10	15	20	25	30	35	40						
90	30		5	10	12	15	20	25	30							
100	25		5	7	10	15	20	22	25							
110	20			5	10	13	15	20								
120	15			5	10	12	15									
130	10			5	8	10										
140	10			5	7	10										
150	5			5												
160	5				5											
170	5				5											
180	5				5											
190	5				5											

From Table 1-11, 1970 *Diving Manual.*

Instructions for Use

I. No-decompression limits:

This column shows at various depths greater than 30 feet the allowable diving times (in minutes) which permit surfacing directly at 60 feet a minute with no decompression stops. Longer exposure times require the use of the Standard Air Decompression Table (table 1-10).

II. Repetitive group designation table:

The tabulated exposure times (or bottom times) are in minutes. The times at the various depths in each vertical column are the maximum exposures during which a diver will remain within the group listed at the head of the column.

To find the repetitive group designation at surfacing for dives involving exposures up to and including the no-decompression limits: Enter the table on the *exact or next greater depth* than that to which exposed and select the listed exposure time *exact or next greater* than the actual exposure time. The repetitive group designation is indicated by the letter at the head of the vertical column where the selected exposure time is listed.

For example: a dive was to 32 feet for 45 minutes. Enter the table along the 35-foot-depth line since it is next greater than 32 feet. The table shows that since group D is left after 40 minutes' exposure and group E after 50 minutes, group E (at the head of the column where the 50-minute exposure is listed) is the proper selection.

Exposure times for depths less than 40 feet are listed only up to approximately 5 hours since this is considered to be beyond field requirements for this table.

Table 9. Surface Interval Credit Table for Air Decompression Dives
[Repetitive group at the end of the surface interval (air dive)]

	Z	O	N	M	L	K	J	I	H	G	F	E	D	C	B	A
Z	0:10 / 0:22	0:23 / 0:34	0:35 / 0:48	0:49 / 1:02	1:03 / 1:18	1:19 / 1:36	1:37 / 1:55	1:56 / 2:17	2:18 / 2:42	2:43 / 3:10	3:11 / 3:45	3:46 / 4:29	4:30 / 5:27	5:28 / 6:56	6:57 / 10:05	10:00 / 12:00*
O		0:10 / 0:23	0:24 / 0:36	0:37 / 0:51	0:52 / 1:07	1:08 / 1:24	1:25 / 1:43	1:44 / 2:04	2:05 / 2:29	2:30 / 2:59	3:00 / 3:33	3:34 / 4:17	4:18 / 5:16	5:17 / 6:44	6:45 / 9:54	9:55 / 12:00*
N			0:10 / 0:24	0:25 / 0:39	0:40 / 0:54	0:55 / 1:11	1:12 / 1:30	1:31 / 1:53	1:54 / 2:18	2:19 / 2:47	2:48 / 3:22	3:23 / 4:04	4:05 / 5:03	5:04 / 6:32	6:33 / 9:43	9:44 / 12:00*
M				0:10 / 0:25	0:26 / 0:42	0:43 / 0:59	1:00 / 1:18	1:19 / 1:39	1:40 / 2:05	2:06 / 2:34	2:35 / 3:08	3:09 / 3:52	3:53 / 4:49	4:50 / 6:18	6:19 / 9:28	9:29 / 12:00*
L					0:10 / 0:26	0:27 / 0:45	0:46 / 1:04	1:05 / 1:25	1:26 / 1:49	1:50 / 2:19	2:20 / 2:53	2:54 / 3:36	3:37 / 4:35	4:36 / 6:02	6:03 / 9:12	9:13 / 12:00*
K						0:10 / 0:28	0:29 / 0:49	0:50 / 1:11	1:12 / 1:35	1:36 / 2:03	2:04 / 2:38	2:39 / 3:21	3:22 / 4:19	4:20 / 5:48	5:49 / 8:58	8:59 / 12:00*
J							0:10 / 0:31	0:32 / 0:54	0:55 / 1:19	1:20 / 1:47	1:48 / 2:20	2:21 / 3:04	3:05 / 4:02	4:03 / 5:40	5:41 / 8:40	8:41 / 12:00*
I								0:10 / 0:33	0:34 / 0:59	1:00 / 1:29	1:30 / 2:02	2:03 / 2:44	2:45 / 3:43	3:44 / 5:12	5:13 / 8:21	8:22 / 12:00*
H									0:10 / 0:36	0:37 / 1:06	1:07 / 1:41	1:42 / 2:23	2:24 / 3:20	3:21 / 4:49	4:50 / 7:59	8:00 / 12:00*
G										0:10 / 0:40	0:41 / 1:15	1:16 / 1:59	2:00 / 2:58	2:59 / 4:25	4:26 / 7:35	7:36 / 12:00*
F											0:10 / 0:45	0:46 / 1:29	1:30 / 2:28	2:29 / 3:57	3:58 / 7:05	7:06 / 12:00*
E												0:10 / 0:54	0:55 / 1:57	1:58 / 3:22	3:23 / 6:32	6:33 / 12:00*
D													0:10 / 1:09	1:10 / 2:38	2:39 / 5:48	5:49 / 12:00*
C														0:10 / 1:39	1:40 / 2:49	2:50 / 12:00*
B															0:10 / 2:10	2:11 / 12:00*
A																0:10 / 12:00*

Repetitive group at the beginning of the surface interval from previous dive

From Table 1-12, 1970 *Diving Manual.*

Instructions for Use

Surface interval time in the table is in *hours* and *minutes* (7:59 means 7 hours and 59 minutes). The surface interval must be at least 10 minutes.

Find the *repetitive group designation letter* (from the previous dive schedule) on the diagonal slope. Enter the table horizontally to select the surface interval time that is exactly between the actual surface interval times shown. The repetitive group designation for the *end* of the surface interval is at the head of the vertical column where the selected surface interval time is listed. For example, a previous dive was to 110 feet for 30 minutes. The diver remains on the surface 1 hour and 30 minutes and wishes to find the new repetitive group designation: The repetitive group from the last column of the 110/30 schedule in the Standard Air Decompression Tables is "J." Enter the surface interval credit table along the horizontal line labeled "J." The 1-hour-and-30-minute surface interval lies between the times 1:20 and 1:47. Therefore, the diver has lost sufficient inert gas to place him in group "G" (at the head of the vertical column selected).

*Note.–Dives following surface intervals of *more* than 12 hours are not considered repetitive dives. *Actual* bottom times in the Standard Air Decompression Tables may be used in computing decompression for such dives.

Table 10. Repetitive Dive Timetable to Air Dives

Repetitive groups	Repetitive dive depth (ft) (air dives)															
	40	50	60	70	80	90	100	110	120	130	140	150	160	170	180	190
A	7	6	5	4	4	3	3	3	3	3	2	2	2	2	2	2
B	17	13	11	9	8	7	7	6	6	6	5	5	4	4	4	4
C	25	21	17	15	13	11	10	10	9	8	7	7	6	6	6	6
D	37	29	24	20	18	16	14	13	12	11	10	9	9	8	8	8
E	49	38	30	26	23	20	18	16	15	13	12	12	11	10	10	10
F	61	47	36	31	28	24	22	20	18	16	15	14	13	13	12	11
G	73	56	44	37	32	29	26	24	21	19	18	17	16	15	14	13
H	87	66	52	43	38	33	30	27	25	22	20	19	18	17	16	15
I	101	76	61	50	43	38	34	31	28	25	23	22	20	19	18	17
J	116	87	70	57	48	43	38	34	32	28	26	24	23	22	20	19
K	138	99	79	64	54	47	43	38	35	31	29	27	26	24	22	21
L	161	111	88	72	61	53	48	42	39	35	32	30	28	26	25	24
M	187	124	97	80	68	58	52	47	43	38	35	32	31	29	27	26
N	213	142	107	87	73	64	57	51	46	40	38	35	33	31	29	28
O	241	160	117	96	80	70	62	55	50	44	40	38	36	34	31	30
Z	257	169	122	100	84	73	64	57	52	46	42	40	37	35	32	31

From Table 1-13, 1970 *Diving Manual.*

Instructions for Use

The bottom times listed in this table are called "residual nitrogen times" and are the times a diver is to consider he has *already* spent on bottom when he *starts* a repetitive dive to a specific depth. They are in minutes.

Enter the table horizontally with the repetitive group designation from the Surface Interval Credit Table. The time in each vertical column is the number of minutes that would be required (at the depth listed at the head of the column) to saturate to the particular group.

For example: The final group designation from the Surface Interval Credit Table, on the basis of a previous dive and surface interval, is "H." To plan a dive to 110 feet, determine the residual nitrogen time for this depth required by the repetitive group designation: Enter this table along the horizontal line labeled "H." The table shows that one must *start* a dive to 110 feet as though he had already been on the bottom for 27 minutes. This information can then be applied to the Standard Air Decompression Table or No-Decompression Table in a number of ways:

(1) Assuming a diver is going to finish a job and take whatever decompression is required, he must add 27 minutes to his actual bottom time and be prepared to take decompression according to the 110-foot schedules for the sum or equivalent single dive time.

(2) Assuming one wishes to make a quick inspection dive for the minimum decompression, he will decompress according to the 110/30 schedule for a dive of 3 minutes or less (27 + 3 = 30). For a dive of over 3 minutes but less than 13, he will decompress according to the 110/40 schedule (27 + 13 = 40).

(3) Assuming that one does not want to exceed the 110/50 schedule and the amount of decompression it requires, he will have to start ascent before 23 minutes of actual bottom time (50 − 27 = 23).

(4) Assuming that a diver has air for approximately 45 minutes bottom time and decompression stops, the possible dives can be computed: A dive of 13 minutes will require 23 minutes of decompression (110/40 schedule), for a total submerged time of 36 minutes. A dive of 13 to 23 minutes will require 34 minutes of decompression (110/50 schedule), for a total submerged time of 47 to 57 minutes. Therefore, to be safe, the diver will have to start ascent before 13 minutes or a standby air source will have to be provided.

Table 11. Theoretical Altitude Dive Tables

Actual depth	Theoretical depth at various altitudes (in feet)									
	1,000	2,000	3,000	4,000	5,000	6,000	7,000	8,000	9,000	10,000
0	0	0	0	0	0	0	0	0	0	0
10	10	11	11	12	12	12	13	13	14	15
20	21	21	22	23	24	25	26	27	28	29
30	31	32	33	35	36	37	39	40	42	44
40	41	43	45	46	48	50	52	54	56	58
50	52	54	56	58	60	62	65	67	70	73
60	62	64	67	69	72	75	78	81	84	87
70	72	75	78	81	82	87	91	94	98	102
80	83	86	89	92	96	96	103	108	112	116
90	93	97	100	104	108	112	116	121	126	131
100	103	107	111	116	120	124	129	134	140	145
110	114	118	122	127	132	137	142	148	153	160
120	124	129	134	139	144	149	155	161	167	174
130	135	140	145	150	156	162	168	175	181	189
140	145	150	156	162	168	174	181	188	195	203
150	155	161	167	173	180	187	194	202	209	218
160	166	172	178	185	192	199	207	215	223	232
170	176	182	189	196	204	212	220	228	237	247
180	186	193	200	208	216	224	233	242	251	261
190	197	204	212	220	228	237	246	255	265	276
200	207	215	223	231	240	249	259	269	279	290
210	217	225	234	243	252	261	272	282	293	305
220	228	236	245	254	264	274	284	296	307	319
230	238	247	256	266	276	286	297	309	321	334
240	248	258	267	277	288	299	310	323	335	348
250	259	268	278	289	300	311	323	336	349	363

Prescribed depth	Theoretical depth of decompression stop (in feet)									
	1,000	2,000	3,000	4,000	5,000	6,000	7,000	8,000	9,000	10,000
0	0	0	0	0	0	0	0	0	0	0
10	10	9	9	9	8	8	8	7	7	7
20	19	19	18	17	17	16	15	15	14	14
30	29	28	27	26	25	24	23	22	22	21
40	39	37	36	35	33	32	31	30	29	28

From E. R. Cross, 1970.

Review questions for chapter 5

1. What are the causes, symptoms, and treatment of decompression illness?
2. Exercise during decompression will appreciably reduce the chance of getting decompression sickness. True or false?
3. The slowest area in the body from which inert gas is eliminated on decompression is
   (a) fat
   (b) blood
   (c) muscles
   (d) skin tissue
4. Give two symptoms for each of the following.
   (a) CNS decompression illness
   (b) Joints (decompression illness)
   (c) Respiratory system decompression illness
   (d) Skin decompression illness
5. Explain how the following contribute toward decompression sickness.
   (a) Fat
   (b) Exercise
   (c) Alcohol
   (d) Smoking
   (e) Fatigue
   (f) Exertion
   (g) CO_2
6. Explain the effects of aseptic bone necrosis.
7. What percentage of the symptoms of decompression illness will occur in the first half hour? After six hours?
8. What are the three principles on which Haldane based his decompression theory?
9. A diver has dived to 100 feet for 25 minutes. One hour later he is flying at an altitude of 7,500 feet and experiences pain in his shoulder. What is the most likely problem?
10. Give at least three contributory factors to decompression illness.
11. Fill in the following using the U.S. Navy Dive Tables.
    70 feet, 70 minutes D.C. ____Group ____
    Surface interval 2 hours   Group ____
    72 feet, 45 minutes   D.C. ____Group ____
12. 80 feet, 30 minutes D.C.____ Group ____
    Minimum surface interval ____Group ____
    60 feet, 30 minutes, no decompression   Group ____

13. 60 feet, 50 minutes D.C. ____ Group ____
    Surface interval 2 hours   Group ____
    ____ Maximum depth for 15 minutes bottom time, no decompression
14. 80 feet, 70 minutes D.C. ____ Group ____
    3 hours surface interval   Group ____
    60 feet, ____ maximum time, no decompression
15. You only have Table 1-5 and make the following dives. What is the safe decompression procedure?
    100 feet, 40 minutes   D.C. ____
    Surface interval 2 hours   Group ____
    100 feet, 20 minutes   D.C. ____
16. 180 feet, 10 minutes. On ascent you have a delay of 5 minutes at 160 feet.   D.C. ____ Group ____
17. 90 feet, 30 minutes   D.C. ____ Group ____
    5 minutes surface interval   Group ____
    90 feet, 20 minutes   D.C. ____ Group ____
18. 210 feet, 20 minutes   D.C. ____ Group ____
    Minimum recommended surface interval ____
    210 feet, 20 minutes   D.C. ____
19. 8 a.m., 120 feet, 30 minutes   D.C. ____ Group ____
    Surface interval ____ Group ____
    12:00 noon, 60 feet, 30 minutes   D.C. ____ Group ____
20. 20 feet, 50 minutes   D.C. ____ Group ____
    Surface interval 1 hour   Group ____
    40 feet, 70 minutes   D.C. ____ Group ____
    Surface interval 30 minutes   Group ____
    30 feet, 60 minutes   D.C. ____ Group ____
    Surface interval 1 hour   Group ____
    60 feet, 50 minutes   D.C. ____ Group ____
21. You have double 70-cubic-feet tanks, fully charged, and your breathing rate is .5 cubic foot per minute. What is your maximum safe bottom time at 100 feet?
    What is your decompression? Repetitive group?
22. A diver dives to 100 feet and his total decompression time is 27 minutes and 40 seconds. What is his bottom time? What are his decompression stops? Two hours later he has 100 cubic feet of air and dives to 132 feet. Assuming his breathing rate at the surface is .5 cubic feet per minute, what is his maximum bottom time? His decompression?
23. A diver accidentally surfaces from a dive to 200 feet for 5 minutes.

What would be a safe procedure for him to follow, if he has not developed symptoms of decompression illness?

24. A diver completes a 160 foot dive after a bottom time of 15 minutes. What is the minimum surface interval he can have to be in repetitive group C?

25. A dive is made to 150 feet for 7 minutes, with a surface interval of 6 minutes. The diver again enters the water and takes 6 minutes to drop to 150 feet where he remains for 10 minutes. What is his decompression?

26. A diver makes a dive to 153 feet for 15 minutes. On ascent he delays at 100 feet for 10 minutes. What are his decompression stops?

27. A dive is made to 100 feet for 21 minutes with an ascent rate of 100 feet per minute. What is the decompression schedule for this dive?

6

Psychological Aspects
of Diving

The psychological adaptions and control needed for safe diving include more than screening divers for claustrophobia and other phobias. The psychological aspects of diving involve personal philosophy, buddy awareness, responsibility, stress, and dive planning. Our discussion will involve psychological prerequisites and adjustments for diving, stress and its avoidance in diving, and safe-diving philosophy.

Psychological Prerequisites and Adjustments for Diving

Unfortunately today many organizations and instructors promote the belief that anyone can dive. As a pure statement this is true. However, if we qualify the statement by saying that anyone can dive safely, it becomes a false statement. There is a difference between breathing underwater under ideal conditions and diving. Things can happen fast underwater, and an ideal situation can change rapidly to a hazardous one. A diver should be capable of dealing with most natural environmental problems. The individual who just swims underwater, however, sometimes finds himself in a situation beyond his control and may become a diving casualty. In our opinion the majority of the population is capable of becoming safe divers under normal diving conditions, and perhaps over half of the population is capable of developing the control and abilities to cope with all diving environments to which they could be exposed. We base this statement on the fact that a diver should possess both common sense and physical ability. Much weakness in either of these areas should disqualify the diver. If a ratio were suggested it should be 60% common sense to 40% physical ability with a 50:50 ratio being acceptable, but not a 70:30 or 40:60. Individuals who are claustrophobic should not be accepted as diving students, and individuals who display other phobias should be observed closely. Diving candidates should be mature individuals (not measured in age but in emotional control) who possess a reasonable degree of self-discipline coupled with some individualism. In diving courses training exercises should emphasize teamwork and buddymanship, yet at the same time enable the diver to become self-reliant. Individuals who always have excuses, or who just simply do not have the drive or self-discipline to accomplish basic skills (underwater swims, ditch and donns, etc.), definitely should be disqualified. There are contradictions to every rule, but individuals who cannot swim at least marginally well should not be accepted in a diving class because they most likely will not have the confidence to contend with adverse situations.

The sad part of training an individual who is not a swimmer is that he usually becomes a dependency diver and cannot fend for himself or assist a buddy under stressful situations. Furthermore, he does not know how to use his muscles (kicks, etc.) in the water; thus, he must receive much more personal attention or he will never really master propulsion skills. On the other hand it is not necessary to be a competitive swimmer to dive, and the minimum swimming requirements spelled out by the Young Men's Christian Association (YMCA) and the National Association of Underwater Instructors (NAUI) are adequate for sport diving. Individuals entering more advanced forms of diving should also possess better watermanship.

The neophyte diver faces a set of new and unusual conditions. He must learn to breathe underwater through his mouth via mechanical devices (regulators); he has to accept that his life support systems have limited durations; he is subjected to physiological hazards; he must learn to breath underwater without a mask; and he must adapt to all the equipment necessary to complete his life support system. Although to experienced divers these steps sound trivial, to many people first taking up scuba they represent major adaptations. Other, more-subtle adjustments are also involved, such as forcing the respiration to remain slow and easy when feeling tense and "uptight." On the surface the natural reaction would be to breathe rapidly so the system could have a greater oxygen uptake.

Obviously, much self-discipline must be mastered during the training phase of diving, and common sense must be developed. The individual with little self-discipline and self-confidence is not going to be as responsive or capable as other persons who already have developed these traits.

An individual who generally displays erratic behavior or "flies off the handle" easily should be discouraged from diving. This type of person usually lacks the control to think his way out of a stressful situation or through his erratic behavior pattern may routinely place himself and other divers in embarrassing predicaments.

Diver Stresses and Avoidance

In the water almost all activities are based on the time allowed by the air supply the diver is carrying. Many other stressful situations, some obvious, some subtle, can occur to the diver. Awareness of these stresses can enable one to cope with them. Robert Smith (4) of American Research Associates explained stress in divers in a most interesting method. According to his breakdown, sources of stress include time pressure, task loading, exertion and cold, directional requirements, buoyancy problems, ego threat, and physical threat.

Time pressure, as mentioned earlier, is an indirect stress to which the diver is always subjected. He is always in a race with the clock to complete his objectives within the time allotment of his air supply. When something slows down his progress, he can be placed under stress. Even the act of getting ready on a rocking boat rapidly and correctly is a source of time pressure stress.

Task loading is the act of having a person attempt to perform more tasks than he can handle. The more work that has to be performed during the dive, the more likely this form of stress may be encountered. If the work is greatly varied, the variety itself can be a source of stress to the diver.

Exertion and cold result in more mistakes and give rise to sensations of discomfort and anxiety. In addition to physical stress it also causes mistakes in judgment and a tendency to rush the job. Rushing a job then causes more mistakes and may lead to a bad situation psychologically.

Directional requirements involving mistakes in navigation, especially on night dives, can result in an uptight feeling. Other sources of directional stress range from simple disorientation to loss of direction due to current. Perhaps the most serious stress involved with direction is when the individual thinks he is lost and begins to question his natural instincts although they are still working well. This leads to disorganization and ends in circular swims. In open water this problem can be coped with by surfacing and reorientating one's self. On decompression dives, saturation dives, or cave dives, however, the surface for practical purposes is nonexistent.

Buoyancy problems cause discomfort and a feeling of being ill at ease because the diver is working too hard. Hard work, of course, increases respiration and shortens air duration. The diver should adjust his buoyancy for neutral when swimming and switch to negative or positive buoyancy as required for accomplishment of his work.

Ego threat is one of the most serious problems facing the diver. If one's ego, that is, his self-evaluation, is threatened, he can become unglued quite rapidly. This condition is the reason why a man may push himself beyond reasonable limits.

Physical threat is obvious. If a diver's welfare is threatened by marine life or other factors he may become very apprehensive.

All the above are stress-triggering mechanisms that can either be controlled or that can lead to panic. Under stress the diver frequently ceases to think logically. He will say "I have a problem," instead of determining why he has a problem. If this tendency is not checked it may lead to panic. Panic is the time when all logic and mental control is lost and only flight remains. A panicked diver is almost impossible to assist and definitely not capable of overcoming the situation.

Psychologically panic is comparable to air embolism physiologically, in that panic is about the worst thing that can happen to the diver, yet it, like air embolism, can be prevented. Panic can be prevented through self-discipline, anticipation, overtraining, and determination of the exact situation. To incorporate these principles divers should strive to develop self-discipline through training and practice. Forethought (anticipation) should be given to any imaginable problem that may arise during the dive. Through overtraining or total familiarity with diving skills most situations can be coped with easily. This includes total familiarization with both your own equipment and that of your buddy. When a problem arises the first instinct should not be an explosive reaction but rather a short delay where thought is given to exactly what the problem is and how best to cope with it. In other words: stop, think, react. Energies should be aimed at solving problems, not worrying about them. Figure 23 summarizes stress reactions.

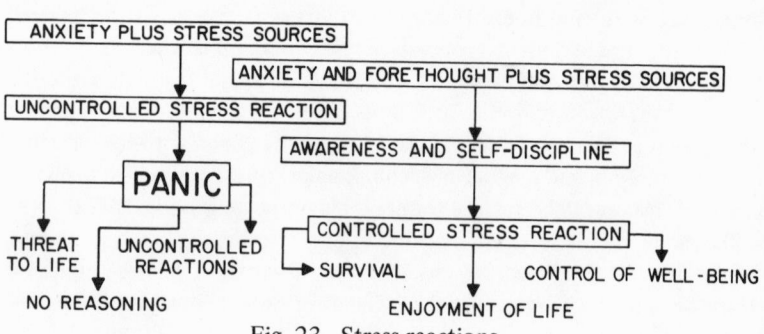

Fig. 23. Stress reactions.

Safe Diving Philosophy

A safe philosophy is mandatory for successful diving. The safe philosophy includes self-honesty; assumption of responsibilities, defensive buddy concept, and dive planning.

Self-honesty

This is a valuable asset to anyone and especially to a diver. The diver who is honest with himself is less subject to ego threat and is more dependable. This diver has an inner awareness of his capabilities and limitations on a daily basis. He does not brag or overrepresent himself, and he establishes a safe personal diving criterium. This does not mean he limits his capabilities; it does mean that he establishes a safety criterium and remains within it, e.g., the dive may become longer and more involved as he gains experience but he still observes the same safety margins or the dives are extended due to his improved performance and possibly more advanced life support systems. By being self-honest the diver also gains the respect and confidence of his fellow diver.

Assumption of responsibilities

Among divers this term includes personal responsibility, buddy responsibility, and responsibility to the diving community. When these responsibilities are accepted, the diver can become a safe diver. The responsible diver follows safe dive habits, remains constantly aware of his buddy, and places his work or research second to human safety. This diver is willing to see that other divers he associates with follow safe diving habits.

In diving, perhaps more so than any other activity, the actions of one diver can affect the reputation of and respect for the entire diving community. Each diver should look at himself as a diplomat or public relations representative of diving.

In research this attitude is magnified greatly since the amount of information attained has to be weighed against safety as well as cost. If human life is jeopardized by failure to follow safe diving habits, it is difficult to justify the research performed.

Defensive buddy concept

This concept is the most valuable contribution to diving. It must be understood that a buddy system is not just two people who are diving together, it is two responsible divers functioning as a unit. Buddy teams should consist of two people who have mutual respect for and confidence in each other.

An effective buddy system ensures that each diver is totally familiar with both sets of equipment. The distance between the divers should not exceed half the range of visibility. When in clear water, the distance between buddies should not exceed a distance greater than half the distance they can swim, after exhalation, from one another. Forethought is given to each dive, and a pace is maintained that does not fatigue the diver or cause him to waste energy reserves needed to respond to an emergency. Stressful situations are avoided or controlled by teamwork and buddy awareness. For example, if a buddy team is collecting samples, and one diver checks his air pressure gauge and finds he has only 500 psig while his buddy has 1,200 psig, there are two choices available. Both choices mean discontinuing the dive. The diver can use his remaining air and then buddy breathe because there is no other choice (except free ascent); in this instance stress will be real. The second choice, and a safer one, would be for the divers to commence buddy-breathing right away and conserve the air of the diver with low air to use should other situations occur (forethought and anticipation incorporated into the dive) when ascending. This type of buddy system is always on the defense against being forced into a stressful situation.

Dive planning

Planning is the key to safe diving and the accomplishment of work. The dive plan must be flexible and not a fixed objective. This does not imply that the dive plan should not include a set amount of work to be accomplished; it means that the plan is made to accomplish the work, but is not inflexible. Although it sounds like a small point, this flexibility is a vital part of a dive plan. When fixation is incorporated into the plan, divers often fail to respond to instinctive warnings that should cancel the dive. The flexible plan says, "let's attempt to accomplish this goal, but if anyone feels uncomfortable or if unexpected conditions arise, then the dive will be stopped at that point."

A good dive plan is one that is agreed on by all partners, incorporates a built-in safety margin, and does the following:

Considers the ability of the least-qualified diver in the group
Anticipates possible problems
Establishes a maximum depth and bottom time
Determines the air used turnaround point
Appoints a dive master
Evaluates all environmental conditions to be encountered
Sets the maximum number of divers and defines their responsibilities

Most of the preceding steps are included in the four primary points of a good dive plan: information gathering, group planning, individual planning, and self-preparation. In addition, dive planning does not stop when one enters the water. A dive plan is a continuous process of reevaluation, orientation (navigation), and updating of vital information. Obviously a successful dive plan therefore must be carried out by alert divers.

Air planning is an area of dive planning worthy of further discussion. The type of dive and diving environment will dictate which general air used turnaround rules are to be followed. The following are general rules for specific dives; they are flexible due to specific environmental differences.

2/3 rule = With the 2/3 rule 2/3 of the air is used during dive performance and 1/3 is used for return to the boat. This rule is used when work is performed upstream of the diving platform (boat, land mass, etc.) and horizontal distances do not exceed 500 feet. Also it should only be used on dives that do not require decompression.

1/2 - 200 rule = With the 1/2 - 200 rule the air is divided into halves and then 200 psig is subtracted as the turnback point. For example, the diver starts with 2,600 psig broken into two segments of 1,300 psig; then 200 psig are subtracted from the second 1,300, so the diver actually will turn back to the boat when his air pressure gauge reads 1,100. Thus 1,500 psig are used during the dive and 1,100 for the return to the dive platform. This rule applies when going upstream and on dives with no decompression.

1/2 rule = The 1/2 rule is applied on short decompression dives or on dives without decompression when current is absent and the dive encompasses moderate swim distances.

1/2 + 200 rule = The 1/2 + 200 rule is used on cave dives or internal wreck dives with outflow current. It is also used in open water dives requiring moderate decompressions.

1/3 rule = The 1/3 rule is used in caves or on wrecks with no current or when work must be performed down current of the boat.

A general statement concerning air planning should include:

(a) On decompression dives the diver should always arrive at decompression with at least one-third of his original air supply.

(b) Upon completion of a dive, the diver should surface with a minimum of 300 psig, with 500 psig recommended.

(c) All air planning should be governed by the first diver reaching the air turnaround point.

(d) The most important factor in a dive is that enough air be held in reserve to cover any unusual situations that may be encountered.

A comparison of the optional air turnaround points is shown in Table 12.

Table 12. Comparisons of Optional Air Turnaround Points

Begin-ning psig	1/3 rule		1/2 + 200 rule		1/2 rule		1/2 – 200 rule		2/3 rule	
	T.A.*	A.U.†	T.A.	A.U.	T.A.	A.U.	T.A.	A.U.	T.A.	A.U.
2,200	1466	733	1300	900	1100	1100	900	1300	733	1466
2,400	1600	800	1400	1000	1200	1200	1000	1400	800	1600
2,600	1732	866	1500	1100	1300	1300	1100	1500	866	1732
2,800	1866	933	1600	1200	1400	1400	1200	1600	933	1866
3,000	2000	1000	1700	1300	1500	1500	1300	1700	1000	2000
3,200	2132	1066	1800	1400	1600	1600	1400	1800	1066	2132

* T.A. = point of turn around in psigs or amount of air left for returning to dive platform.

† A.U. = amount of air in psigs used up to the time of turning back.

Review questions for chapter 6

1. List three psychological adjustments that must be made when one enters the water.
2. List the three major responsibilities of a diver.
3. Match the following:
   - (a) Buddy team
   - (b) Dive plan
   - (c) Live and let live
   - (d) Self-honesty

   - (1) Earn respect and give respect
   - (2) Two individuals diving together
   - (3) Sets definite objectives
   - (4) Leave others alone and be left alone
   - (5) Establishes maximum desired performance
   - (6) A unit acting as one force
   - (7) Knowledge of one's limitations
4. On a dive with a new buddy, you should dive up to your limitations and depend on him to establish his limits. True or false?
5. Circle the three most pertinent factors in developing a good philosophy for diving.
   - (a) Good technique
   - (b) A working approach to dive planning
   - (c) Assumption of responsibilities
   - (d) Extreme self-confidence
   - (e) Physical to mental relationship
   - (f) Psychological adjustments
6. The ideal common sense to physical ability ratio is
   - (a) 50:50

   (b) 60:40

   (c) 40:60

   (d) 70:30

7. List three new conditions to which the new diver is exposed.

8. List three sources of stress in diving.

9. A safe diving philosophy includes four things. What are they?

10. Define the defensive buddy concept.

11. List the four primary points of a good dive plan.

12. List the five common air turnaround rules and an example of where each would be used.

7

Accident Prevention and Management

Scuba accidents are usually discovered as a result of drowning, decompression sickness, air embolism or forms of barotrauma, and injuries due to marine organisms. Many accidents are not reported, however, and frequently complications result from mismanagement. Accidents usually occur following one or more critical incidents. The most obvious way to avoid accidents is to avoid incidents leading up to them.

As indicated by the title, this chapter is divided into two categories, prevention and management. Prevention is the key word and requires research into several aspects of diver history: emotional and physical stability and conditioning; degree of training and diver education; type of equipment used and familiarity with it; the three development stages of a diver; and physical and psychological stress.

Prevention

Emotional and physical stability and conditioning

Once man leaves his natural habitat he must be emotionally and physically competent to meet the demands placed on him in a new environment. A balance in emotional and physical stability and condition cannot be overemphasized.

In considering the emotional fitness of a diving candidate, three factors come into play: common sense, maturity, and self-discipline. Individuals weak in any of these areas should be disqualified from participating in diving activities.

Common sense is the ability to reason and make calm logical decisions. Employment of common sense enables the diver to think ahead and avoid compromising situations. This is perhaps the most important trait of a diver, but unfortunately, it is frequently overlooked in diver selection and qualification.

Maturity is a broad term, expressing a complete physical and/or mental development. A mature individual is competent to base decisions on all pertinent factors and admit to his limitations. Self-honesty is perhaps the most important measure of maturity. Being self-honest entails accepting one's limitations and communicating these to associates who rely on him. The diver who is honest with himself can control his ego and avoid placing himself or others in situations beyond their abilities. The most important aspect of self-honesty is that it enables one to fulfill the three responsibilities of a diver. These are the responsibilities to himself, to his buddy, and to the entire diving population. When a diver considers these responsibilities and not just his individual desires, he is mature.

Self-discipline is the ability to enforce decisions based on maturity and common sense. A diver who has mastered self-discipline is capable of controlling physical and emotional response to a hazardous situation. Most diving instructors are aware of the importance of self-discipline and plan many training exercises to develop this trait.

The need for physical stability and conditioning should be obvious at this point. A diver does not have to be in top athletic condition, but he should be a competent swimmer and relaxed in the water. At least an average degree of coordination is mandatory, and the stamina to react to environmental demands must be present. A diver with little coordination or who is totally "out of shape" simply will not be capable of responding to the many environmental demands that may be placed on him. Ignoring the need for physical ability or conditioning frequently results in the diver being placed in an embarrassing situation.

Degree of training and diver education

The next step in accident prevention is diver training and education programs. Diver training is a broad term encompassing more than just teaching someone to propel himself with swim aids and breathe underwater. An understanding of diving physiology and physics coupled with relaxation, good judgment, and awareness should be essential parts of a scuba course.

It is unfortunate that many programs seem to emphasize quantity of students instead of quality. This illogical approach is stimulated by competition among instructors and certifying bodies, potential sales by dive shops, and (not least) by instructors who are not fully aware of the seriousness of diving themselves.

Type of equipment used and familiarity with it

Equipment to be used should be adequate for the dive planned. The diver should be totally familiar with the equipment and its proper operation. Often divers have all the desired equipment but lack the familiarity to make it function correctly. When equipment changes are made, the diver should make a few easy familiarization dives with it under ideal conditions.

Buddies should be familiar with each other's equipment so that no wasted time is encountered in event of an emergency situation.

The three development stages of a diver

As divers evolve from the status of basic to accomplished divers they go through several stages of development. For simplicity's sake we will discuss only three of these stages: basic, intermediate, and accomplished.

For preventing accidents, an understanding of these stages and their impact on accident probability is mandatory. The basic diver if unattended and left to fend for himself is the most likely suspect for an accident. The well-trained basic diver realizes he is not sufficiently proficient and usually employs caution to as great a degree as possible considering that many things in his new environment will be totally foreign to him (even with good training). Overall though, he will employ caution in his diving and most likely will dive with persons of greater experience for a few dives at least. During the first five to ten dives the basic diver is comparable to a baby walking for the first time, but after a few dives he develops his confidence and abilities to the point that he becomes competent.

As skill development continues the diver enters the second and perhaps the most hazardous phase of his diving career, the intermediate stage. Most divers enter this phase somewhere between 15 to 25 dives and remain there until 40 to 100 dives have been made. The reason that this stage of diving is so conducive to accidents is that during this period the diver's abilities in the water have developed at a rapid rate, he probably has experienced a couple of minor incidents that were potentially dangerous (buddy breathed because of necessity or encountered his first shark). It is at this time that his self-confidence may exceed his physical and emotional abilities. During this period it is desirable for the diver to be introduced to experienced cautious divers or, ideally, for him to be utilized in assisting with diver training programs. As an assistant he can develop a sense of responsibility that will enable him to adjust his own advancement pace.

The final stage of development is that of the accomplished diver. At this stage the diver is least likely to be involved in accidents. As in aviation, however, divers in this stage go through several periods in which they are more prone to accidents than at other times. Most periods of higher accident probability are due to the diver's negligence of minute details and a feeling of being able to handle virtually any situation he may get into. Fortunately the diver in this stage of diving, even when going through one

f the higher critical incident periods, usually has enough background to
avoid serious accidents.

Physical and psychological stress

Physical and emotional stress are major contributions to accidents. Stress
is a stimulus that involves threat to a diver's welfare. Perhaps the most
dangerous point about stress is that it can be such a subtle occurrence and
can develop gradually. Stress can also occur suddenly and explosively,
depending on the situation and possible anxiety of the diver.

Physical stress is invoked by such environmental factors as cold, unnoticed degrees of narcosis that affect our physical responses, and fatigue.
The effects of physical stress have been well documented by Glen Egstrom
and other investigators.

Psychological stress is of major importance to divers and offers an
interesting study in natural reactions that are apparently intended as fight
instincts but which act as self-destruct mechanisms in the water. One
example of a survival reaction that is threatening in the water is the release
of adrenalin with corresponding increases in respiration and heartbeat. The
increased respiration presents a threat to the diver in that it means increased air consumption and breathing patterns that will result in respira-
ory distress, due to turbulent airflow in the airways of a diver.

To control stress one must learn to cope with critical incidents that
could develop into accidents. Several approaches are available for this
purpose: thinking ahead about the dive, establishing preconditioned reflexes, and utilizing the overtraining process in diver training programs.
When in an uptight situation the diver should stop, breathe, relax, think,
and then react. A diver should not react explosively and instinctively
without thinking through the situation.

Accident Management

As previously explained, accidents are managed best by preventing circumstances leading up to them. All such circumstances cannot be avoided,
however, and human error will always result in some accidents.

The most common diving accidents are drowning, decompression sickness, air embolism, injuries, and fatalities.

Drowning is the most frequent diving accident and can result from a
variety of reasons, e.g., running out of air, overexertion, injury, or panic.
The immediate consideration is not why the accident occurred, but rather
how to save the victim's life. It should be noted that why is important and
must be known to prevent future accidents. But why can be discovered
after proper first aid or medical attention is given. The drowning victim

should be surfaced in a safe manner to prevent air embolism. Methods of surfacing unconscious divers vary, but two seem to be most logical and popular. The first of these entails surfacing the victim with his head held back, opening the airway, and depressing his diaphragm until the victim has surfaced. When using this technique the rescuer should adjust both his and the victim's buoyancies to neutral (by use of the buoyancy compensator). On ascending the buoyancy compensator may be deflated enough to prevent too rapid or uncontrolled ascent. The second method of surfacing is to bring the victim up feet first. Regardless of method, once on the surface the victim's buoyancy should be positive, and the rescuer should also have slightly positive buoyancy.

On the surface, the victim's mask is discarded, and the rescuer may put his own mask on his head. The victim is now lying with his head back and airway open. By tilting the victim's head to the side $15°$, resuscitation can be administered without ducking him or inducing water into his airways. The victim is given mouth-to-mouth resuscitation for 1 minute; then if no help is available, he is towed to the boat as follows: two to four strokes and one ventilation. The process is repeated until arrival at the boat. Once the victim is in the boat, resuscitation is continued, and cardiopulmonary resuscitation (CPR) procedures are begun if necessary. The Coast Guard or other rescue services are called. As always, first aid should continue until medical help is available or death has been confirmed.

The next most common accident is air embolism. This problem is always suspect when an unconscious diver is discovered. It may vary from a passive victim on the bottom to the classical case of the victim surfacing, exhaling, and becoming unconscious. In the water, ascent is performed as previously described and mouth-to-mouth resuscitation is given if needed. Once out of the water the victim should be placed with his head down and preferably with his left lateral side down. (A tilt board is recommended.) If needed, resuscitation is administered, and the victim should breathe oxygen if available. The Coast Guard should be contacted (Highway Patrol, et cetera, if inland), and the victim should be rushed to the nearest recompression chamber. At the medical facility the diving conditions and symptoms should be described to the medical advisor.

Decompression sickness is becoming common in many areas of the United States due to poor decompression technique or lack of knowledge on the part of the diver. A victim should be kept quiet, observed for shock, given proper first aid if needed, and the Coast Guard or other similar rescue agency should be notified. If oxygen is available, it should be given to the victim until help arrives. He should then be transported to

he nearest chamber for treatment. Under no circumstances should drugs
or pain relievers be administered until the victim is under medical care.
uch drugs could hide symptoms that would be decisive in the selection of
reatment tables.

Respiratory-induced accidents are common contributors to many other
liver accidents. A few factors to be considered in these accidents are the
ncreased density of air at depth, mechanical breathing resistances peculiar
o the equipment, the amount of work performed, and the possibility of
arbon dioxide buildup. Correct breathing patterns in a diver are manda-
ory. The saying "just breathe normally" is not really applicable for diving.
he statement must be qualified because almost every principle of normal
espiration is deviated in diving, for example, in diving breathing is through
he mouth instead of the nose.

Effective breathing patterns must be established to minimize the effects
of turbulent airflow in the diver's airways (deadspace) and to maximize
entilation of the lungs. Usually, slow, deep breathing is considered the
most efficient method of breathing in scuba. Another important factor is
stablishing an ideal work and breathing balance point. Work requirements
ot balanced with the ventilation criteria of the diver or breathing patterns
esulting from stress stimuli will result in one of the following: uninten-
ional hypoventilation, extreme skip breathing, failure to exhale, or an
verload on the breathing apparatus. Obviously each of these conditions
an rapidly create a critical incident and develop into an accident.

Extreme skip breathing may result in excessive carbon dioxide (CO_2)
etention, which will produce symptoms of confusion, headache, drowsi-
ess, and possible loss of consciousness. Although it is true that this in-
rease in CO_2 tension will tend to stimulate the respiratory center and
stablish better ventilation, a diver under stress may override this stimulus.
Another possible alternative is that by the time the diver does give in to
he CO_2 stimulus respiration may become rapid and shallow thereby pro-
lucing turbulence in the airways and ventilation will be restricted. In
ddition to restriction of ventilation due to turbulent gas flow, the diver
vill be in a state of hypoventilation.

Unintentional hypoventilation may result due to a stress stimulus.
ymptoms of this condition include weakness, numbness, faintness, blurry
ision, a feeling of suffocation. This can lead to further problems such as
evere hypocapnia associated with muscle spasm, loss of consciousness,
nd shock. This condition is also further complicated by turbulence in the
liver's airways.

Failure to exhale sounds unlikely and "way out" to many divers. Yet under stress it is a possible and probable reaction. Frequently a novice diver will surface and complain that his regulator does not work, and upon examination the regulator is usually found to be in excellent working order. This reaction is usually triggered by a stress stimulus. What happens is the diver inhales a deep breath and perhaps may exhale a small portion of the air, inhales deeply again, and continues the cycle until he is no longer able to take more air into his lungs. To the affected and nonthinking diver, the problem is identified as equipment malfunction, which may produce even more stress reactions. This individual is the one who signals to buddy breathe but is unable to do so due to failure to exhale. Symptoms consist of confusion and erratic motion. As both hypercapnia and hypoxia set in, the diver may exhibit symptoms of confusion (he becomes unable to concentrate), loss of muscle control, emotional instability, and faulty judgment. He may even begin to feel good and then black out. Pulse rate is increasing; however, the condition is so subtle that to the diver himself it may be hard to identify.

The last abnormal breathing pattern that may occur due to stress is to overdemand the breathing apparatus. This may occur as a result of hard physical exertion or because of faulty design of the breathing apparatus.

The thinking diver is aware of these possible changes in breathing under stress. To control them, he disciplines himself to adjust his breathing to his workload and vice versa, and when under stress he conditions himself to stop physical activity, exhale fully, and resume a correct breathing pattern. In our opinion many diving accidents are caused by failing to breathe correctly and by allowing oneself to fall unknowingly into one of the discussed breathing patterns. Indeed, this possibility may offer an explanation for why many divers, though highly experienced and professional, drown with tanks one-third to almost completely full. After reviewing the accident reports of many drownings, we have found that the typical symptoms dicussed above were described by the surviving witness. These breathing problems are not suggested as the conclusion for "why" these accidents occurred, but only, as a possible cause and a theory for further research. Further support for this approach can be gained when one considers that these conditions themselves may produce more stress in addition to the stress stimulus that initiated them. If complicated by problems such as inert gas narcosis and dense gas in the breathing medium of the diver, with increased respiratory work, a clear picture of a dangerous closed-loop system can be envisioned.

Hyperventilation can result in becoming light-headed and unconscious. When a diver becomes aware that he is hyperventilating, he should cease activity and control his respiration (employ slow and deep breaths). Extreme skip breathing results in a carbon dioxide buildup and can have end results similar to those of hyperventilation. Again the diver should concentrate on establishing good ventilation. An excessive demand on the breathing apparatus can result in hyperventilation or cause the diver to feel he is not getting enough air, thereby placing him under stress. Efficient work requires either short bursts of energy and a breathing break or slow, continuous work. The work load should not consist of steady, hard work unless in free flow or commercial equipment. Fast, hard, physical labor should always be avoided. In normal diving, the diver should avoid swimming fast; instead, he should concentrate on developing an efficient slower pace that avoids "overwork," which in the end results in a greater air versus distance ratio.

Accidents can be prevented or correctly managed through good training programs and periodic reviews of first aid practices. The latter is a function that each dive council or club should include among its duties.

Review questions for chapter 7

1. Give two reasons that should be grounds for discouraging individuals from diving.
2. Three factors should be considered in determining emotional fitness of a diving candidate. Define each of these.
3. Name the three development stages of a diver.
4. List five steps a diver in an uptight situation should undergo.
5. Name the most common diving accidents.
6. Explain why effective breathing patterns are important in prevention of diving accidents.

Physical Performance and Different Diving Environments

In addition to psychological evaluation and knowledge of physiological hazards, man must be physically fit and must develop physical skills to be efficient in the water. Although common sense is the most important part of a diver's makeup, it can truthfully be said that "the physically unfit individual is unfit for diving" and "the nonthinking diver is noncapable." It is not necessary to be a real Tarzan to dive, but a reasonable degree of physical fitness is needed. The unfit diver will not be capable of responding to situations even though he may be a logical thinker. Exercises such as jogging, swimming, tennis, volleyball, and so on, should be undertaken as a means of conditioning by divers. *Skin Diver* magazine has featured many editorials using statistics and summaries of early season diving accidents to emphasize two points: the importance of physical conditioning, and the knowledge of daily limitations and staying within them.

A physically fit individual is more ready to face abnormal situations in the water. A bull plowing through the water, however, instead of gliding with the water, is soon going to exhaust himself and his buddies. There is a lot to be said for the statement "if you are going to be a diver, look like a diver." To look like a diver, one must be graceful and smooth. This is accomplished by maintaining good body positioning by use of buoyancy control, swimming at a relaxed pace, and by incorporating good diving skills and techniques. Variations in the diving environment will dictate which techniques provide the most efficiency and safety.

Physical Performance

When considering physical performance in the water, the diver must develop a reasonable ratio of air used versus distance traveled, avoid excessive drag by proper trim, employ correct techniques for the type of dive to be performed, and select equipment that will enable him to accomplish safe physical performance.

The combination safety vest/buoyancy compensator is an absolute must for the research diver. Most techniques involving good trim or changes from swimming buoyancy/trim to working buoyancy cannot be accomplished efficiently without this device. Other equipment considerations are adequate air supply, weight belts, protective clothing, and a well-designed regulator or breathing medium.

General physical performance can be discussed in reference to buoyancy control and body positioning and to hand and kicking techniques.

Buoyancy control and body positioning
This aspect is most important for developing good technique. Factors that control these two functions are equipment design, negative or positive buoyancy, and the type of kicks used. In general, the diver should strive to present as smooth a profile in the water as possible. A diver swimming with his feet down creates more drag by having to push more mass through the water, and in this attitude he is probably negatively buoyed so that he must work harder. This causes increased air consumption and the possibility of respiratory embarrassment. A diver in a head-down attitude is most likely positively buoyed and is working hard to stay down, creating more drag in the water by his increased frontal area. Positive or negative buoyancy when making forward progress is unacceptable for underwater swimming. It will be shown later that there are times when both positive and negative buoyancy are incorporated into the swimming technique.

Neutral buoyancy is the ideal condition toward which to strive, and through proper use of weights and the buoyancy compensator it is obtainable. (See Figure 24 for comparisons of body positions.)

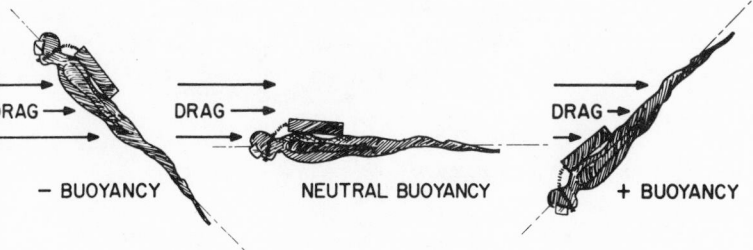

Fig. 24. *Left to right:* Negative buoyancy, neutral buoyancy, positive buoyancy.

By maintaining proper body positioning and controlling buoyancy the diver can propel himself through the water with minimum effort. Thus the air used versus distance traveled ratio is increased. Proper use of the buoyancy compensator enables the diver to attain neutral buoyancy for swimming, negative buoyancy for work, and variable buoyancy for ascent or for assisting a disabled diver.

Hand and kicking techniques

These techniques are used to develop propulsion. Any technique used should minimize effort, maximize distance per energy expenditure, and maximize efficiency. All techniques will incorporate neutral, positive, or negative buoyancy. Almost all techniques incorporate neutral buoyancy. The following is a breakdown of common techniques.

Standard open water. Neutral buoyancy and a full flutter kick are utilized in the standard open water kick. The body is in a horizontal position. The kick travels almost equal distance above and below the midline of the body as in Figure 25.

Fig. 25. Standard open water kick.

Modified open water. This abbreviated open water kick is used whenever there is sediment on the bottom and it is desired not to disturb it. The kick is identical to the standard open water kick except that the downstroke does not exceed $10°$ below body midline (see Figure 26).

Fig. 26. Modified open water kick; the downstroke must not exceed $10°$ below midline of body.

Shuffle kick. This kick utilizes neutral buoyancy. On this technique one flipper acts as a shield and the other is brought from up high down to the shield. Legs can be rotated. This is an efficient technique and it is especially good for not disturbing the bottom sediment (see Figure 27).

Fig. 27. Shuffle kick.

Bottom pull. The bottom pull incorporates a slight negative buoyancy and is most effective for use in heavy current or when leg cramps develop. It as the name implies is simply pulling along the ocean floor. It can be modified by pulling on ledges, etc. (see Figure 28). The bottom pull can also be used in conjunction with any of the other kicking techniques when appropriate.

Fig. 28. Bottom pull.

Dolphin neutral. Buoyancy should be neutral whenever the dolphin kick is used. The legs and feet are held together, the back is arched, bringing the upper body and feet upward. Thrust is gained by the down-stroke of the legs and the body leveling. This stroke resembles the butter-fly stroke except that the arms are not used.

Modified frog kick. The modified frog kick is used in conjunction with neutral buoyancy. With this kick the knees are out and the flippers are heel to heel. The kick is out to the sides and back together. This is a good trade off kick to use when switching from one kick to another, and it is excellent for not disturbing the bottom (see Figure 29).

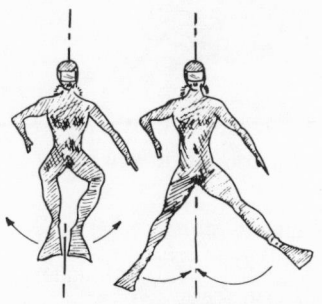

Fig. 29. Modified frog kick.

Bottom pull, heel walk. The bottom pull, heel walk is used under ledges or in enclosed environments, primarily against the current. With a slight positive buoyancy and the feet elevated, the diver pulls along the ocean floor and walks with heels of flippers along the overhead projection (see Figure 30).

Fig. 30. Bottom pull heel walk.

There are many other techniques available, but mastery of these should give the diver the basic techniques to cope with most environments. There is one other technique that should be mentioned for use when carrying heavy objects along the bottom.

Angle walk. The angle walk is used to carry heavy objects along the ocean floor for short distances or when working with surface-supplied equipment. The diver executes the angle walk by removing his flippers, picking up the heavy object, and leaning slightly forward and walking. Sometimes this technique is called moon walking because of its unusual stability characteristics and the fact that leaps can be utilized (see Figure 31).

Fig. 31. Angle walk.

Different Diving Environments

In addition to general open water techniques, some environments require special study. The structure or the key life of some environments must be understood to avoid accident or injury. Areas of special emphasis are those dealing with certain forms of marine life, diving in current, cave diving (freshwater and ocean blue holes), ice diving, wreck diving, saturation diving, and surf.

Marine life

Certain forms of marine life must be understood to prevent injury. This text will not offer a complete discussion on marine life, but our discussion is intended to deal with those that bite, those that sting, those that cut, and those that poison.

Under the category of those that bite, only marine life that is a potential threat will be discussed. The most commonly feared predator is the shark. All sharks are potential threats to man; however, some species such as the white, mako, et cetera, are of more concern. By displaying a calm attitude and employing common sense we can make most encounters with sharks inconsequential. The diver should observe the shark for erratic behavior, such as humping, rapid movements, et cetera. Sharks displaying unusual behavior should suggest that the diver seek cover and leave the water at the earliest convenient time. When sharks are encountered the divers should remain in a horizontal position and not upright. Leaving the water should not be attempted when a shark displaying erratic behavior is in the immediate area. (There are of course conditions that cause exceptions to this rule.) Physical contact with the shark should be avoided. If a shark attack does occur, first aid for bleeding and shock should be administered immediately and medical help sought. In general, if diving is to be performed in the ocean, the fact is that a shark will be seen sometime during the diver's career. Although sharks are a potential threat, they are not swimming diver eaters, awaiting the unwary individual.

Barracuda offer another source of old wives' tales as to their insatiable appetite for divers' fingers and legs. Investigation reveals that few documented attacks on divers by barracuda exist, although all divers in tropical waters are exposed to them routinely.

Moray eels are also biters, and again there are few documented, unprovoked attacks from these capable creatures. The moray is so dangerous that many divers hand-feed them. Attacks from morays can be avoided if respect is extended to morays and their territory.

All three of these so-called "bad guys" have reputations that far exceed their activities. We do not mean that they are not potentially dangerous, because they are. If common sense is employed, however, the chances of being attacked by any of these species is quite remote. Again, if attack does occur the first aid is to control bleeding, treat shock, resuscitate if needed, and seek medical attention. The greatest danger is not from being eaten, but from bleeding to death and from shock, with the secondary danger of infection.

A wide range of animals that sting is encountered. These animals are more common causes of injury and agony than any other one category. Of this category we will discuss only the more common causes of agony to man: Portuguese men-of-war, fire coral, jellyfish, sea urchins, toxic sponges, and poisonous fish. For the first three of these, the first aid is to break down the protein of the stinging cells. Ammonia and water, alcohol, and meat tenderizer are all good for this purpose.

Many people are highly allergic to Portuguese men-of-war, and here there is the chance of shock and even death, so prompt medical attention is recommended for allergic reactions. A good immediate first aid procedure is to use foam and shave the affected area. Other sources of agony or great concern are scorpion fish, zebra fish, lion fish, et cetera. It is recommended that all divers refer to one of the many excellent books on these species for further knowledge and identification purposes.

In the category of marine life that cuts, barnacles are the primary concern. The greatest threat is one of infection, and prompt first aid is needed.

Various species of nonpoisonous fish can be poisoned by eating certain poisonous fishes or algae. Many fishes are known to carry toxins, and others, due to their food chain, are edible only in some areas. The diver should know which fish can be eaten and which cannot. He should check with local residents when visiting areas outside his normal residency. The astute diver acquaints himself with area fish and toxicity prior to arriving in a new area.

Sea snakes and other dangerous species exist in the Pacific and Indian oceans and are documented well beyond the scope or intent of this text. Marine life is discussed here only to acquaint divers with the potential hazards and to stimulate further individual investigation.

Diving in current

Diving in current is a condition that the diver frequently encounters. When diving in current we must consider anchoring, setting up the boat, and dive technique. Frequently, divers not familiar with current diving bail overboard and to their dismay are swept down current. This condition can be avoided through awareness, self-discipline, and the incorporation of special techniques.

The first consideration is anchoring the boat. When possible two anchors should be set with adequate scope (five to seven times water depth). A stern line attached to a float should be extended 200 feet aft of the boat. A descending line should be lowered, preferably amidships, from the boat to approximately 6 feet above the bottom. When really strong currents exist or the anchor line is used to serve as a descending line, an entry line is used. The entry line is fixed either to the bow, the anchor line, or the descending line. This line is grasped by the diver, in such a way that he does not become entangled as he enters the water. The purpose of the line is so the diver is not swept away upon entry into the water and so he can pull himself up to the descending line. (See Figure 32 for illustration of boat and lines.)

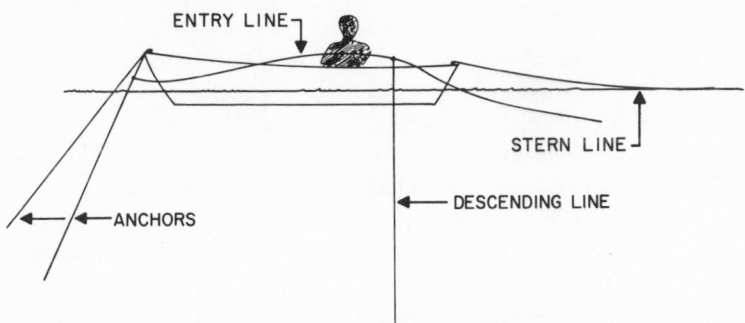

Fig. 32. Lines in relation to boat.

One person must be in the boat at all times to act as safety man. If divers are below and a troubled diver or divers surface and cannot make the safety line, the bow anchors are attached to a buoy and set free after the motor is started but out of gear. The boat will now drift. Once clear of the dive area, the motor is put in gear and the divers picked up. Upon return, the boat hangs off the marker buoy that was attached to the anchor line until an O.K. signal is received from the remaining divers. The boat then proceeds to go upstream of the buoy and feed out its safety line so that the remaining divers can depart the anchor line and grasp it. At this point the boat can drift while the divers pull up and get on board or it can drift back to the anchor buoy and be secured to it while the divers are boarding. The second method is preferred (see Figure 33).

A diver leaving the boat should maintain contact with the entry line (if used) and pull up to the descending line, then descend to 10 feet and await his buddy. Descent should be made hand over hand down the line. Contact should not be lost with the descending line even momentarily.

On the bottom if the current still prevails the bottom pull technique should be incorporated in conjunction with the kick technique of the

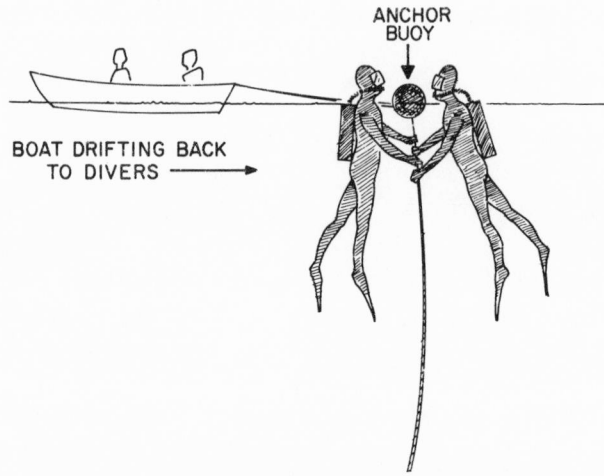

Fig. 33. Recommended method for picking up divers.

diver's preference. Ascent should also be hand over hand, and the diver should remain on the descent line or stern line until his buddy is completely on board the boat. Under no condition should a diver hang directly below the ladder or diving platform. When exiting via ladder, the diver should hang onto the ladder, remove his flippers, carry them in his hands, and keep the regulator in his mouth and mask on until onboard the boat. The logic behind this method of exiting is that (1) removal of flippers reduces possibility of tripping, plus ensuring that if the diver does fall he does not get a broken leg due to the blade of his flipper hanging up in the ladder rungs; (2) flippers are kept in the hands so that they can be used if the diver does fall back in; (3) regulator remains in the mouth so that the diver can breathe if he falls back into the water; (4) mask is left on for vision. This technique should always be applied when using a dive ladder. When we use a dive platform, flippers are kept on until on board.

Cave diving

Cave diving is performed both in freshwater and in salt water. Due to its inherent hazardous conditions, that is, no free ascents, et cetera, specialized training is a must prior to engaging in this form of diving. Many caves, such as the Blue Holes of the Bahamas, have their own specific problems. In these caves there is a tidal current reverse that occurs two to four hours after tide changes, dependent upon location. One reverse is an outflow, the other is an inflow, so one could say the caves act as both a spring and siphon system dependent on time.

In cave diving, special emphasis should be given to life support systems, dive planning, and philosophy, as well as specialized techniques.

Whenever man enters the water he is dependent on mechanical devices for his survival. In cave diving this dependency is amplified more than in any other form of diving. A minimum life support system for cave diving must include the following.

1. Propulsion and visual system (mask and fins)
2. Exposure suit
3. Diver ventilation system (Air dives require single 71.2 cubic foot tank or larger and single hose regulator with octopus or quadrupus system; deep dives or long exposures require a properly designed mixed gas rebreather)
4. Navigation aids (safety reel and line, compass, and modified outrigger clasp)
5. Buoyancy control devices (weight belt and buoyancy compensator vest)
6. Underwater lighting system (primary and secondary)
7. Knife
8. Decompression monitors (watch, depth gauge, submersible dive tables)
9. Slate and pencil
10. A logical diver

In cave diving the diver is frequently carrying more equipment than normal and often is swimming against strong currents. To offset this workload, serious consideration should be given to using power fins. These fins give greater power and due to their slower kicking rate generate less silt than swim aids. The mask should be of low volume but still offer a good visual field.

The water temperature and marine organisms will determine the necessary protective clothing. In warm blue holes, the diver may wear only a sweat shirt and pair of gloves, whereas in colder water he may wear either wet suits, dry suits, or wet-dry suits.

Since man must have a breathing supply for survival, selection of this system deserves much emphasis. When using open-circuit scuba, the tanks selected must be adequate to supply air for the duration of the anticipated dive. Tanks used vary from single 71.2 cubic foot tanks to double 100 cubic foot tanks.

For long-duration dives, double tanks are normally selected. The method of use of doubles and added safety has been debated very much in diving, and the following recommendations are made as a result of trial and error evaluation of each system. Recommended systems are ideal manifold, permanent manifold, temporary yoke, and two separate tanks. See Figure 34 for all the tank configurations.

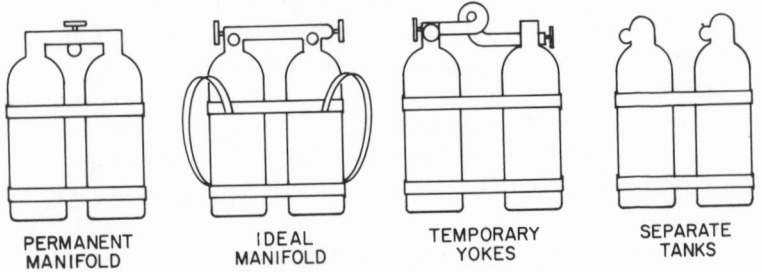

PERMANENT MANIFOLD   IDEAL MANIFOLD   TEMPORARY YOKES   SEPARATE TANKS

Fig. 34. Four types of double-tank setups.

The ideal manifold is one whereby two banks are manifolded together, making the air supply common but offering two regulator outlets. The advantage of this system is obvious—should a malfunction occur, one regulator may be shut off, while the other has the full volume of air available to it.

The permanent manifold is the most commonly used system and has proved to be safe when used with an octopus system.

Many divers choose to yoke two single tanks together with a temporary yoke. For open water diving this system has many advantages. Structural weakness and critical alignment of tanks make this system questionable for use in the cave environment. Inherent disadvantages include blowing tank O rings when the yoke is bumped on a cave ceiling with a corresponding loss of air, and on several occasions the silver solder going into the regulator mounting block has given way when bumped. Most experienced cave divers consider this to be an unsafe system.

Logically speaking, two separate tanks are an attractive system. It is important to note, however, that all cave divers who have tried this system a dozen times or more have come to the conclusion that it rates as being suicidal. Several accidents have been attributed to this system. With this system, the diver must trade regulators midway of the dive, and the system is subject to more regulator failure owing to a possibility of silt in the second stage of the new regulator.

When one chooses a set of double tanks, special consideration should be given to their buoyancy characteristics and maneuverability. The regulator should supply adequate volume and feature low inhalation and exhalation resistance. An octopus system should be utilized (except when the ideal manifold is being used). This system involves attaching an extra second stage and submersible air pressure gauge to the regulator. Octopus systems for cave diving are mandatory because manual buddy breathing is impractical and occasionally impossible due to distance and cave configuration. The air pressure gauge is the only safe method of monitoring air supply. Many divers now use a quadruptus system, which incorporates an automatic inflator for the buoyancy compensator.

Some divers like to carry a buddy tank of 20 to 40 cubic feet mounted between their doubles for emergencies.

One of the inherent dangers of cave diving is becoming lost. To offset this possibility, the diver must use a safety reel and line. A suitable safety reel should feature a line guide, drum, buoyancy chamber, a good turns ratio, and, it should be capable of carrying approximately 400 feet of 1/16-inch, 160-pound test to 1/8-inch, 440-pound test, braided nylon line. The reel should be close to neutral buoyancy, compact, and rugged. (See Figure 35 for navigation aids.)

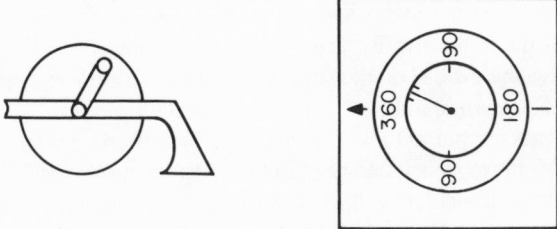

Fig. 35. Navigation aids. *Left,* safety reel; *right,* compass.

A compass is used to avoid disorientation when diving on permanent lines or in the event of line breakage. The compass is also used as a mapping aid.

Outrigger clasps modified with pointers are used when jumping from one line to another. The pointer is aimed in the direction out of the cave (see Figure 36).

Fig. 36. Outrigger clasp and pointer.

Another means of backup cave navigation is referred to as memory referencing. Basically it involves being familiar with cave structure and combining visual referencing.

Two pieces of equipment provide for adjustments in the diver's buoyancy; they are a weight belt and a buoyancy compensator vest.

The weight belt is used to offset the positive buoyancy of the diver, whether due to his natural buoyancy or to that caused by his wet suit or other equipment.

In cave diving most divers prefer to start the dive approximately 3 to 5 pounds negative at the surface, so that at the end of the dive they are neutrally buoyant at the surface. By being so weighted, the diver at 10 feet is still negative enough to be stable during decompression.

As depth is increased, compression of the wet suit causes the diver to become more negative, so a buoyancy compensator vest is used to attain the desired buoyancy condition (usually neutral). The buoyancy compensator vest is also valuable as a buddy rescue device.

The well-designed buoyancy compensator features a small neck, a large air bag, a crotch strap, and a low center of buoyancy. It should utilize an automatic inflator system. By proper buoyancy control the diver reduces drag, increases his air duration, avoids silt, and minimizes exertion.

The light system should consist of a minimum of two lights, a main light (30 watts or better) and a safety light (submersible flashlight). The lights should be rugged, compact, and capable of supplying light for the duration of the dive. Ideally, lights should be easily and quickly recharged.

The knife should be easily accessible, small, and sharp. In cave diving the knife is regarded as a survival tool in the event that the line becomes severely entangled.

To accurately keep track of bottom time, decompression, and depth, the diver must have an accurate depth gauge, a dependable watch, and a set of dive tables.

For communications and recording dive events (bottom time), a slate and pencil are a must.

Perhaps the most important part of any life support system is a diver who thinks logically. The entire life support system is dependent upon the individual's judgment and decisions.

The key to safe cave diving lies in the philosophy of the diver and is reflected in his dive plan. A safe philosophy ensures receiving proper training in cave diving and recognizes the responsibilities the cave diver is subjected to: himself, his buddy, and the diving population. A diver who is first responsible to himself is capable of establishing safe dive limits, being honest with himself, and not ego involved. These traits allow him to recognize the dual responsibility of the buddy system and cause him to be selective in choosing a buddy. By incorporating all this into their dive habits, the buddy team fulfills its responsibility to the diving population by self-policing, setting good examples, and not allowing objectives to outweigh the safety criteria of the diver.

A good rule for a safe dive limit is: do not dive beyond the point where you can assist your buddy or be assisted by him back to the surface.

The dive plan must be flexible, establish an air turnaround point, consider the ability of the least experienced diver, and set the maximum number of divers allowed on the dive. Normally no more than three divers should be on a given dive.

Three special considerations of a dive plan are: acquiring information on physical peculiarities of the cave, establishing communications and understanding of the dive plan, and selecting technique and equipment for the dive.

Each diver should feel free to call (stop) a dive for any reason without a threat of nonacceptance from the other team members.

Special emphasis should be placed on air cutoff planning. Each diver should arrive at the mouth of the cave with a minimum of one-third of his air supply. To do this, there are three general rules:

1. For low outflow caves or new caves use one-third of air going in, allow one-third for coming out, and save one-third for emergencies or decompression.

2. For caves with moderate outflow use two-fifths of the air supply going in and allow three-fifths for the return, decompression, or emergencies.

3. For heavy outflow caves use the $1/2 + 200$ rule. Example: A dive is started with 2,400 psig; the diver can go into the cave until he reaches 1,400 psig at which time he would begin the exit (one-half of $2,400 = 1,200 + 200 = 1,400$ psig).

As in everything, there are exceptions and modifications to the general rules, but any change should allow the diver one-third of his air supply for the unexpected.

To offset the natural hazards of cave diving, which include a ceiling overhead, darkness, visibility, current, and physical peculiarities of the cave, special techniques must be utilized. Perhaps the greatest specific hazard in cave diving is that of silt, and much effort must be made to avoid it.

These special techniques form two general categories: swim techniques and line techniques.

Swim techniques include the buoyancy control, body positioning, and skills utilized by the diver. There are over 40 known and practiced swim techniques in cave diving. Five basic techniques, however, should allow the diver to employ safe swim techniques. These are the flutter kick, the shuffle kick, finger walking, wall pulling, and heel walking with hand pull. Each of these techniques is designed to minimize effort and silting, to be used comfortably, to allow an efficient speed versus air duration ratio, and to allow for a change of pace.

Flutter kick. The flutter kick is perhaps the most familiar of kicking techniques. It is the standard swimming kick used with a crawl stroke. One leg extends upward while the other goes down, the legs passing each other back and forth to propel the diver. For cave diving, the flutter kick is modified in two ways:

1. The diver use a normal flutter kick except that the downstroke does not exceed 10° below the diver's centerline.
2. Flutter positive, the diver maintains slightly positive buoyancy and his kick is the maximum distance away from the floor, this is used in heavy silt and low overhead caves.

Shuffle kick. The shuffle kick is very efficient and aids in silt prevention. It is employed in both the neutral and positive buoyancy attitudes. In large nonsilty caves this kick can be modified so that as the upper fin comes down, the lower fin is lifted till the fins meet. This kick provides a good trade off stroke and is an efficient means of diver propulsion.

Finger walking is employed in caves with low overhead and moderate silt. As the name implies, it means walking on one's fingertips. Special care must be taken to keep the legs lifted high and to avoid dragging knees and equipment on the cave floor (see Figure 37).

Fig. 37. Finger walking.

Wall pulling is used in caves with a heavy outflow current or when conserving air. The diver swims near one wall of the cave and pulls with his hands while kicking.

Heel walking and *hand pulling* involve a technique that can always be relaxing but is primarily intended for use in low-clearance areas with heavy outflow. The technique requires slight positive buoyancy, arching the back so that the feet are on the ceiling and the hands are on the floor where they can grasp and pull on rocks, etc. The diver then walks on his heels and pulls with his hands. Correct selection of the desired techniques requires the cave diver to analyze cave configuration, select correct technique, and employ the technique correctly.

Line techniques involve correct usage of lines to avoid entanglements and prevent line breakage. Lines are either temporary or permanent.

Temporary lines are the most commonly used and consist of a safety reel and line. When running a safety line, the reel man should maintain tension against the reel drum so the line remains taut. The line should be tied within surface light, and two wraps around an outcropping should be made approximately every 100 feet. The line should be centered in the cave as much as possible. The reel man is the first man in and the last man out. The buddy is responsible for unwrapping the safety wraps on leaving the cave and providing light for the man who is tying or untying the line. Physical contact with the line should be avoided except when the cave becomes silted, at which time the diver should make the standard O.K. sign around the line.

Permanent lines are used for complete exploration or mapping of caves. There are four general categories of permanent lines: novice lines, traverse lines, exploratory lines, and offshoot lines.

Novice lines are lines installed in caves where much diving is done. These lines start at the mouth of the cave and extend a distance of 100 to 300 feet into the cave. These lines are usually larger than normal (1/4- to 9/16-inch braided nylon).

Traverse lines are lines intraconnecting two cave openings.

Exploratory lines start approximately 400 feet into a cave and extend for varying distances. When diving on these lines, one should not assume he can reach the end of the lines because some lines may have been put in using larger volume tanks or staged tanks.

Offshoot lines are lines running into tunnels that run off the main tunnel. These lines should never be connected to the main line. They should have a gap of 10 to 20 feet. When diving on offshoot lines, the diver should place the out-rigger clasp with a pointer indicating the direction out on the main line.

In general, the diver should not penetrate farther into a cave than he is capable of forming visual references, and he should not assume that he can swim to the end of any line. The air cutoff point should allow the one-third rule to be incorporated to provide diver safety. Above all else, the diver should employ common sense and seek training prior to entering a cave.

Ice, saturation, and wreck diving

As a general rule safety precautions necessary in cave diving will afford adequate dive safety for ice diving, saturation diving, and wreck diving, but each project and each area will have specialized problems that the diver must familiarize himself with prior to diving. Ice diving especially has much variation in technique among various groups, and the diver must accept these variations, couple them with the other data available (primarily from cave diving), and dive accordingly.

Saturation diving using scuba can be treated almost exactly like the combination of open water and cave diving skills discussed previously. The important consideration is awareness and the acceptance of a theoretical ceiling. Each project will afford familiarization with its specific problems.

Wreck diving is also highly variable, requiring simple basic skills up to and including advanced diving skills. In each field specialized techniques and procedures have been developed, and the diver should acquaint himself with these and follow them.

Surf

To dive in surf the diver must familiarize himself with wave characteristics. The actual method of entry is also variable. Many persons advocate entering the water with all equipment on, backing out to water of knee to thigh depth, then timing the wave frequency and going in during the small-wave period and avoiding breakers. The diver in front of a breaker is in for an experience he will long remember. When a diver visits unfamiliar areas he should consult local divers about their methods.

Review questions for chapter 8

1. Thee things must be analyzed prior to deciding on a given technique. They are:
   - (a) boat configuration, life support system, and buddy
   - (b) current, silt, and bottom time
   - (c) selection of proper technique, correct employment of the technique, and type of dive
   - (d) depth, bottom time, and air duration
2. List four factors to be considered when deciding on which techniques to use.

3. A crotch strap is needed to prevent the buoyancy compensator from riding up on the neck. True or false.

4. Explain the advantages of an automatic inflator attached to the buoyancy compensator.

5. Circle factors that will cause changes in the diver's buoyancy during a dive.
   (a) Wet suit compression
   (b) Wet Suit
   (c) Mask volume
   (d) Changes in air volume in tanks
   (e) Light systems
   (f) Changes in depth

6. Positive buoyancy will result in
   (a) head up trim
   (b) head down trim
   (c) head and body level trim
   (d) depends on type of buoyancy compensator

7. Define air versus distance ratio.

8. Explain how you would plan and perform a dive in heavy current.

9. The most practical method to calculate air used on a completed dive for your own information is _____ . In making comparisons of air consumption between divers with different tank volumes _____
   (a) determine psig used per minute
   (b) determine cubic footage used per minute
   (c) determine total psig used on dive
   (d) determine total cubic footage used on dive

10. The fish that covers itself with sand and that may inflict a painful wound is the
    (a) moray eel
    (b) sand shark
    (c) manta ray
    (d) stingray

11. Sea urchin spines, if broken off in the skin
    (a) may be left in without harm
    (b) should be extracted if possible and the puncture should be treated to prevent infection
    (c) should be dissolved in gasoline
    (d) should be left in but soaked in Epsom salts

12. What type of marine life hazard would the diver most likely encounter in the following areas?

    (a) Pilings and boat hulls
    (b) Murky water where garbage is dumped
    (c) Placing hands in holes in reef in pursuit of lobster

13. What is the correct anchor scope?
14. List the ten parts of a life support system for cave diving.
15. List four methods of connecting double tanks and explain which is the preferred method for cave diving.
16. List orientation aids for cave diving.
17. What is the key to safe cave diving?
18. Give a good definition for a safe dive limit.
19. List the air rules commonly used in cave diving.
20. Give the four natural hazards of cave diving.
21. Explain three techniques used in cave diving and how they are beneficial in other forms of diving as well.
22. What are the two major types of lines used in cave diving?
23. Plan a dive in surf.
24. Plan a night dive.
25. Plan a wreck dive.
26. Plan an ice dive.

Diving Equipment

The safety and comfort of the diver depends on the equipment used. By choosing proper equipment for the type of dive to be performed, man can blend into and with the water, allowing greater efficiency and safety.

The selection and maintenance of equipment normally used by the research diver can be discussed in the following categories: skin diving equipment, accessory equipment, open-circuit scuba, closed- and semi-closed-circuit scuba, and surface-supplied equipment.

Skin Diving Equipment

Skin diving equipment is equipment used for breath-hold diving. It consists of a mask, snorkel, flippers, and a weight belt.

The diving mask creates an air space between the eyes and fluid interchange, therefore enabling the diver to have good vision. A proper mask for diving differs from swimmers goggles in that it covers the nose of the diver so pressure can be equalized and water can be cleared from the mask.

Desirable features in a mask include a low-volume, comfortable skirt, an adjustable head strap, a shatterproof lens secured by means of a metal or plastic band, and a correct fit on the diver. A correctly fitted mask when held up to the face will have no air gaps between the mask skirt and the diver's face. To check the fit, one can press the mask tightly against the face or inhale slightly and the mask should remain on the face momentarily.

Prior to diving, saliva or liquid detergent may be rubbed on the lens and then washed out, to prevent fogging. The straps should not be too tight, or too loose.

Masks should be rinsed with freshwater and stored in a cool, dry place. The life of a mask can be prolonged by the periodic use of a silicone-based grease on the rubber parts.

The snorkel is a tube designed so that a diver can swim face down on the surface and breathe. There are many types of snorkels available, but the basic one is the J snorkel. The curve of the J snorkel should be smooth. A curve too deep will cause excessive clearing and breathing resistance. A well-designed snorkel should also have a comfortable mouthpiece 12 to 14 inches in length and have a barrel large enough to minimize inhalation resistance. The advantage of a big barrel snorkel is that it provides low inhalation resistance while not adding greatly to exhalation resistance. Snorkel care and maintenance is the same as for the mask.

Flippers are used as a means of propulsion in the water. Their purpose is to provide an extension of the leg and foot and to give more surface area when the diver kicks, thereby propelling him further and more efficiently through the water. Three general categories of flippers are available on the market: full foot flippers (shoe fins, often referred to as swim aids); adjustable open-heel strap flippers (also known as intermediate fins); and fixed, open-heel strap flippers (also some adjustable fins, known as power fins, fall in this category. The power rating of flippers depends upon blade area and flexibility. Selection depends on many factors, such as muscle tone in the diver's legs, type of diving, and the physical characteristics of the diver.

When choosing full foot flippers, care must be taken to avoid overly tight or loose flippers. Tight fins will result in cramps, and loose fins will produce blisters. Overall fit should be comparable to that of shoes.

An intermediate flipper is ideal for normal diving because it provides adequate thrust but will not overtax the leg muscles.

Power fins are used frequently by working divers or those divers who are in the water often. It is generally believed that these offer the greatest efficiency to divers who have good muscle tone.

A weight belt carries weights to offset positive buoyancy. The main feature in a weight belt is that it has a quick release buckle. The weight belt is always the last item on and the first off. In case of an emergency, you should be able to ditch it without entanglement.

A weight belt can work two ways. Weights may be added to attain neutral buoyancy for ordinary diving. With a buoyancy compensator weights may be added to attain negative buoyancy for work on the bottom; then the buoyancy compensator may be inflated to attain neutral buoyancy for swimming. Weight belts should be rinsed with freshwater and stored in a cool, dry place.

Accessory Equipment

The accessory equipment used by the diver greatly influences his physical and physiological safety. Most of this equipment is mandatory for safe diving. Special emphasis must be placed on the importance of a good watch, a depth gauge, and submersible dive tables. On dives below 30 feet all three of these items are mandatory. An exposure suit, a buoyancy compensator and safety vest, a compass, a submersible air pressure gauge, and a knife are other important accessories.

The watch is one of the most important pieces of equipment a diver can have. It allows him to track dive time. The watch must be pressure proof, shock resistant, and waterproof.

It is best to purchase a good watch right from the start. Experience has proven that an inexpensive watch is usually more troublesome than it's worth. A good watch is expensive, but at least you are diving instead of waiting for the watch to come back from repairs. An obvious consequence of not having a watch, or having one that is undependable, is an increased probability of decompression sickness.

The depth gauge indicates the depth of the diver and is essential. There are many types of depth gauges, but they come under four general categories: capillary, diaphragm, digital, and Bourdeon tube. Since the gauges have mechanical movements, except for the capillary gauge, and occasionally receive rough treatment, it is a good practice to periodically check their calibration. The only other maintenance needed is to rinse with freshwater.

Submersible dive tables are a must to all divers. A diver can miscalculate his dive plan by going deeper or extending his bottom time. The submersible dive tables can keep him out of trouble by recalculating his dive, providing he knows how to use them.

The importance of the watch, depth gauge, and submersible dive tables is obvious. The watch keeps track of the dive time. The depth gauge records the depth to which the diver has gone. The tables enable the diver to keep out of decompression or to calculate any required decompression.

Exposure suits are worn to protect the diver from the environment and to maintain body heat. Exposure suits then can range from sweat suits, wet suits, dry suits, dry wet suits, to hot-water suits.

Sweat suits are frequently worn in warm waters to protect the diver from cuts, abrasions, stings, and sun. They are not generally used for maintaining body heat.

The wet suit insulates the diver against a cold environment. The suit material is made of closed-cell, unicellular, neoprene foam. A thin layer of water between the body and the suit is trapped and the body temperature warms the water, giving protection against the cold. Since the suit is made up of tiny gas cells, the suit is compressible and loses some of its insulating protection when compressed. This type of exposure suit is the most commonly used and should be custom tailored to the diver. For maximum warmth the wet suit should feature a hood, as it has been observed that as much as 25 percent of the heat loss is due to not having the head and back of the neck covered.

Dry suits are used in extremely cold water and were used before the invention of the wet suit. This suit is completely watertight, and thermal underwear is worn underneath it.

The dry wet suit is ideal for working or diving in cold water. The suit features variable volume, thus the diver can control his buoyancy as well as maintain body heat. The suit is made of closed-cell neoprene rubber and is generally a one-piece suit sealed at both the ankles and wrist. Lightweight or heavy underwear may be worn inside the suit, depending on the water temperature.

Care and maintenance of all suits is to rinse in freshwater, dry and powder the suit, and store it in a cool, dry place.

The combined buoyancy compensator and safety vest is the ideal solution for controlling buoyancy and also for acting as a flotation device for the distressed diver. The simple safety vest was first developed, and it was followed by a buoyancy compensator that did not feature the advantages of a safety vest. Ultimately the two were combined.

The safety vest was originally used for emergencies. When a diver is in trouble, he can inflate the vest to keep himself afloat, until help arrives. The vest features both carbon dioxide and oral inflation. Even though oral inflation was possible, due to low volume, lack of a crotch strap, and difficulty with deflation, the safety vest was not satisfactory as a work tool or a means of buoyancy control.

As time progressed divers realized the vest could be used for purposes other than safety. By increasing bag size and adding a crotch strap, the diver could create a buoyancy compensator. Using this the diver could control his buoyancy and body position, resulting in more efficient swimming and decreased air consumption. There are many pros and cons for both the compensator and the safety vest. The safety vest has limited functions and is worn mainly for emergencies. Buoyancy compensators can be used to control buoyancy and assist distressed buddies.

A vent valve is usually added to protect the compensator from over inflation. The main objection some divers have had against the buoyancy compensator is that there is no way to inflate the compensator in an emergency, because it does not feature carbon dioxide inflation.

The buoyancy compensator and safety vest combination features many new items. These compensators come with one or two carbon dioxide cartridges, and the cartridges come in multiple sizes. Crotch straps hold the vest in position, and a neck strap holds the neck area down, allowing the head to have more mobility.

The preferred color of the vest is yellow or bright orange. These colors can be spotted in open water easily. Black, however, blends into the water, and a diver in distress wearing a black vest is very difficult to locate.

An automatic inflator may be added to the compensator. The automatic inflator hose is connected to the scuba regulator, although the vest can still be inflated orally. This system is mandatory for deep diving. With this system a diver can control buoyancy without having to remove his mouthpiece.

The vest should be rinsed thoroughly with freshwater. The carbon dioxide cartridges should be removed, and the firing mechanisms should be cleaned and coated with silicone grease. The cartridges should be replaced, and the vest should be orally inflated and stored in a cool, dry place.

The compass orientates the diver, allowing him to get back to where he started or to a new location. The compass is also valuable for mapping and surveying. A compass should feature a rotating bezel, marked degrees on the face, a marked lubber line, and a wrist strap. On a compass course in open water with current the diver must compensate for the current to avoid missing his objective. Rough handling of the compass should be avoided. It should be rinsed with freshwater and stored in a cool, dry place.

The submersible air pressure gauge is attached to the high pressure part of a scuba regulator. It indicates the amount of air in the tank. Thus a diver can regulate his dive by the amount of air being consumed. The J reserve gives 300 to 500 pounds of reserve pressure, providing the J is in working order and has not been bumped down. A J reserve will not get a diver back if he has extended his air supply. Gauges should be rinsed with freshwater after each use and periodically calibrated for accuracy.

Open-Circuit Scuba

Open-circuit scuba is the most common equipment used in sport and research diving. Basically speaking, open-circuit scuba consists of an air cylinder and a demand regulator. The air cylinder functions to carry an available air supply for the diver. It is usually a metal container designed to carry high-pressure air. Regulators are designed to reduce high-pressure air to ambient-pressure air (see Figure 38).

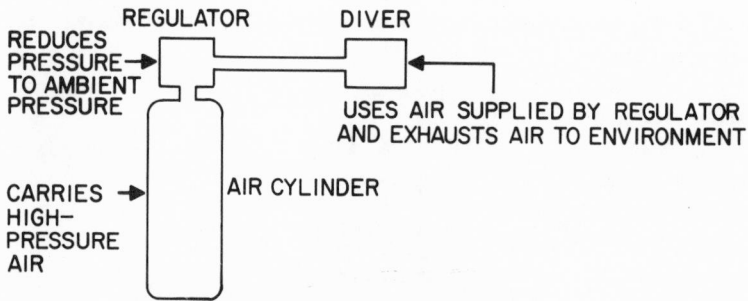

Fig. 38. Open-circuit scuba.

Regulators may be one stage or two stage and either double hose or single hose in design. The following categories of regulators are those generally used.

Double hose, one stage
Double hose, two stage
Standard diaphragm, single hose
Balanced first-stage diaphragm
Flow-into piston, first stage
Flow-through (balanced) piston, first stage

The double-hose, one-stage regulator reduces pressure from tank pressure to ambient pressure in one stage. This is accomplished through the use of an upstream valve and mechanical levers (see Figure 39).

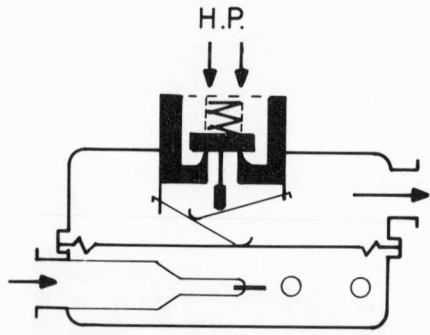

Fig. 39. One-stage regulator.

The double-hose, two-stage regulator uses two stages of pressure reduction. The first stage reduces the pressure from tank pressure to approximately 100 psig; the second stage reduces the pressure to ambient. Usually the first stage is an upstream valve and the second stage is a downstream valve (see Figure 40).

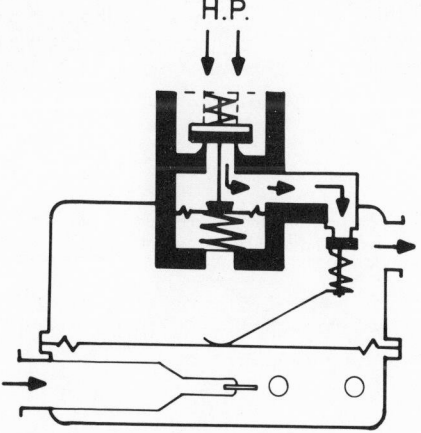

Fig. 40. Two-stage regulator.

The standard diaphragm, single-hose regulator is quite popular in diving circles. The function of the first stage is to allow high pressure to enter through the filter to the high-pressure chamber. The diaphragm and the heavy spring act to force open the high-pressure seat assembly. Pressure enters the intermediate chamber. The diaphragm presses against the heavy spring and compresses it. When the pressure reaches the predetermined pressure of 110-130 psi, the high-pressure seat assembly closes, and will not allow higher pressure to pass. The moment the pressure in the intermediate chamber is reduced by breathing or purging the heavy spring expands against the diaphragm, forcing the high-pressure seat assembly to open. Then the pressure flows through, repeating the cycle. The pressure in the intermediate chamber can be adjusted by the adjustment screw on the end of the heavy spring (see Figure 41).

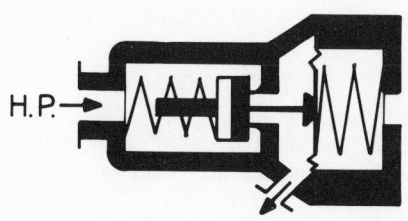

Fig. 41. Standard single-hose first stage.

The second stage may be a tilt valve (upstream) or a fail-safe valve (downstream). There are advantages to both types; however, the tilt valve is not considered to be as safe or reliable as the fail-safe valve. The valve steam in the tilt valve second stage is extended to touch the diaphragm. Whenever the pressure in the breathing chamber is reduced, the diaphragm is forced against the stem, tilting the valve away from the seat and allowing pressure to pass through (see Figure 42).

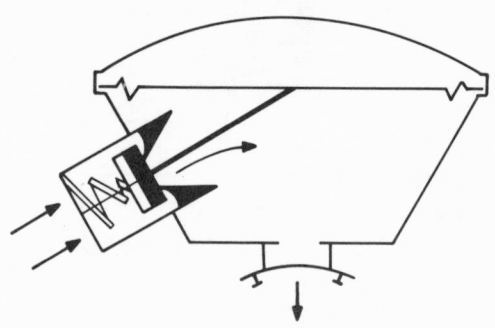

Fig. 42. Upstream valve, second stage.

The major problem with the upstream second stage occurs when the high-pressure seat leaks. The intermediate pressure is greater than normal and tends to close the valve, which causes breathing to become more difficult or impossible. Because of this effect, a safety plug is attached to the low-pressure port to relieve pressure greater than the desired pressure. Safety plugs are not always reliable, however, and when the plug malfunctions the low-pressure hose may rupture.

In a fail-safe (downstream) second stage the pressure pushes the valve away from the seat, opening it. A spring holds the valve seated against intermediate pressure. With a decrease of pressure in the breathing chamber, the ambient pressure is now greater than the pressure inside. The diaphragm comes down on the lever connected to the valve stem, pulling the valve away from the seat and allowing air to flow to the diver (see Figure 43).

The advantage of the fail-safe second stage is increased safety. If the high-pressure seat assembly malfunctions, it will cause an overpressure to the second stage. This pressure pushes the valve away from the seat, causing a free-flow condition. Thus in this regulator a first-stage leak will result in a free flow.

A balanced first-stage regulator provides a greater volume of air to the

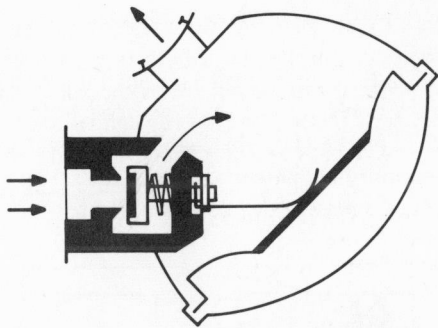

Fig. 43. Downstream valve, second stage.

diver. The major difference between a balanced and a standard regulator is the design of the high-pressure chamber. In the balanced regulator the chamber is like a box; the valve stem extends through the chamber and utilizes an O ring seal. The operation of the regulator is very much the same as the standard, except for the high-pressure seat assembly.

In the standard regulator, the high pressure enters the chamber and the force is directly on the valve. With the balanced first stage, however, the high pressure enters the chamber and the pressure is distributed equally around the valve. As the regulator is cycling there is very little friction against the valve. Therefore, with the movement of the high-pressure seat assembly minimized, the regulator will deliver a greater volume of air to the diver. The adjustment for the intermediate chamber is the same as for the standard regulator (see Figure 44).

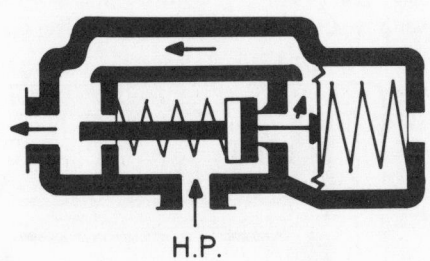

H.P.

Fig. 44. Balanced first stage.

The flow-into piston, first-stage regulator has several advantages over the standard first stage. The most significant advantage is that it has only two moving parts—the piston and the spring. The spring is preset, and no adjustment is made to the intermediate pressure. The piston is hollow and has two small holes at the stem. The high-pressure seat assembly is also part of the piston.

The pressure goes through a small hole in the piston into the intermediate chamber. As pressure increases and the piston compresses the spring to its preset compression, the high-pressure seat assembly closes. The moment the intermediate pressure reduces, the spring expands and the pressure flows in, thus repeating the cycle (see Figure 45).

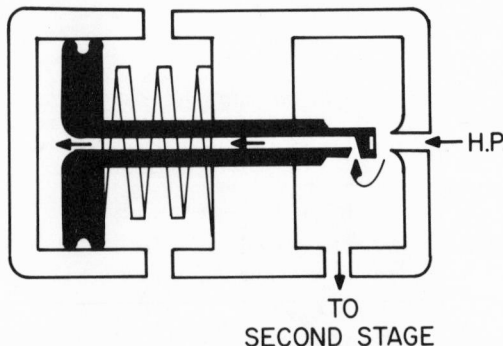

Fig. 45. Flow-into piston.

The flow-through piston is a balanced first stage. The piston and the spring action are the same as in the flow-into piston. The characteristics of the pressure flow are different; instead of the flow going into two small holes, it goes through the piston from one end through the other directly to the second stage. The bore of the piston is also larger in size, which means it will deliver a greater volume of air to the diver (see Figure 46).

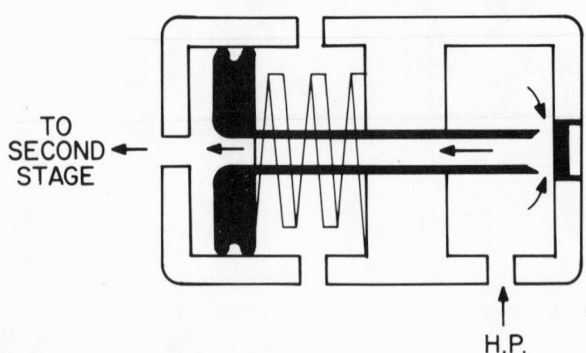

Fig. 46. Balanced flow-through piston.

The octopus system is a regulator with one first stage and two second stages and a submersible air pressure gauge. This system allows easier buddy breathing by allowing the divers to each have a second stage. By not having to pass the regulator back and forth, there is less chance of stress or panic due to becoming winded or uptight. If this type of regulator were used more often, many accidents could probably be avoided. For deep diving, diving in confined spaces, or diving with students or novice divers, this system is a must for safety.

Many divers modify the octopus system to a quadrupus system by adding an automatic inflator for their buoyancy compensator. The advantages of the quadrupus are many. The greatest advantage of this system, however, is that the diver's life support system always remains intact, i.e., he does not have to remove the regulator from his mouth for buddy breathing or to inflate his buoyancy compensator.

Care and maintenance of regulators consist of rinsing with freshwater and periodic maintenance and repair by an authorized repairman.

Tanks

Scuba tanks are used to carry an air supply for the diver, and the tanks come in both steel and aluminum models. In addition to different metals, sizes of tanks also vary, ranging from low volume to high volume. Obviously, in order to contain the volume of air needed the tanks must be charged to high pressure. The working pressure (operational pressure) is the pressure at which the tank contains its rated volume. The working pressure varies from 1,800 psig to 6,000 psig.

The neck of each scuba bottle is stamped similar to the following (see Figure 47):

DOT—stands for the Department of Transportation. This is the agency that sets the safety standards on all high-pressure vessels. Prior to 1970, this service was provided by the Interstate Commerce Commission.

3AA—used to describe the metals used in the tank or, in the event of aluminum, this number may be SP6498. The SP stands for special permit and 6498 is the number given to Alcon Aluminum.

2250 (can be anywhere from 1800 to 6000)—the working pressure of the tank.

CKD—the manufacturer's symbol.

123456—the serial number of the tank.

11 ⬨N 73 + —the stamp explaining the tank was hydrostated (pressure tested) in the eleventh month of the year 1973. The ⬨N is the symbol used for the hydrostatic agency. A plus (+) following the

hydrostat date means the tank can be pressurized to 10% over its working pressure. The plus only occurs on steel tanks.

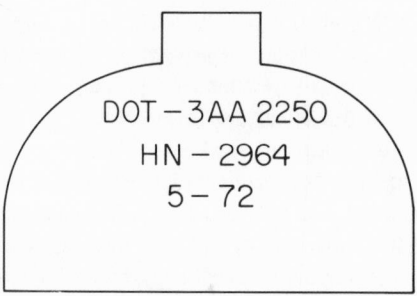

Fig. 47. Sample cylinder identification.

By law, high-pressure tanks must be hydrostated every five years. Hydrostating is accomplished by placing the tank in a sealed, water-filled container and pressurizing the tank with water. The pressure applied to a tank will be 5/3 the working pressure, i.e., a tank rated at 2,250 would require a hydrostat pressure of 5/3 of 2,250 = 3,750 psig. Due to this pressure, the tank will expand displacing water into a calibrated tube (gauge) (see Figure 48).

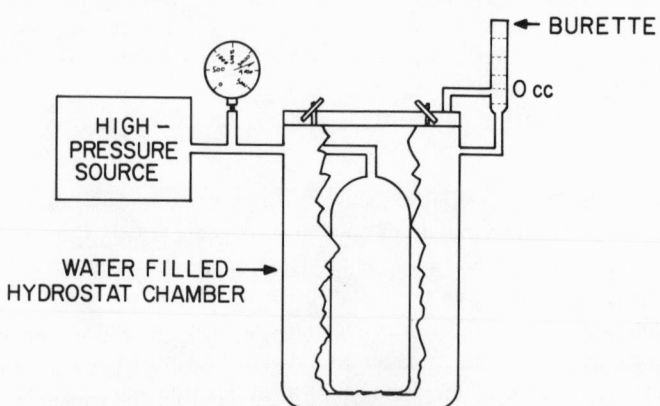

Fig. 48. Expansion of high-pressure cylinder displaces water, forcing water into the burette.

Once the pressure has stabilized, a reading is taken from the tube and the pressure is released. After tank pressure is returned the zero psig, another reading is taken from the tube. If the tank comes back to 10% of its original size or no more than 10% of its total expansion, the tank then passes the hydrostat test.

In addition to hydrostatic testing, steel scuba tanks must be visually inspected annually on a visual inspection program (VIP). It would be a good practice, although it is not mandatory, to inspect aluminum tanks as well. The purpose of the visual inspection is to look for rust or pitting in steel tanks. Rust or pitting can weaken or destroy a steel tank, and tanks must be visually inspected to safeguard them against these occurrences. If rust or pitting is found, the tank should be cleaned either chemically or by a tumbler. Excessive corrosion, even if cleaned, is grounds for hydrostating the tank. Aluminum tanks are usually inspected for aluminum oxide. To prevent corrosion in tanks, they should never be drained of air. When tanks are drained for flying, etc., then care should be taken to close the valve and get the tank filled as soon as possible.

Tanks should be stored in an upright position since the metal thickness is greater at the top and bottom of the tank (see Figure 49).

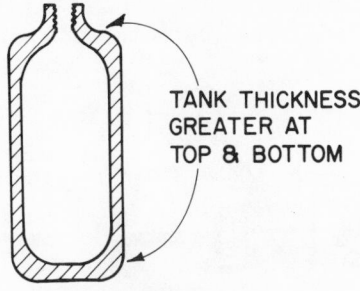

TANK THICKNESS
GREATER AT
TOP & BOTTOM

Fig. 49. Store tanks upright since metal is thicker
at top and bottom of tank.

As stated earlier, the tank is a vessel to carry high-pressure air for the diver to use. Obviously, there must be some way to keep the air in the tank or to release it to the regulator. To accomplish this, tanks are fitted with valves. The valve may be a simple on and off valve, such as the K valve, or a spring-loaded reserve valve known as a J valve (pictured in Figure 50).

A J valve uses a spring-loaded mechanism to allow the diver reserve air. Usually the reserve is approximately 300 psig. In this valve, the seat

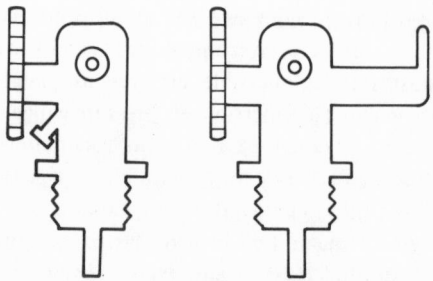

Fig. 50. Two types of valves. *Left,* K valve; *right,* J valve.

assembly is downstream of the tank pressure. A spring acts to hold the valve open. As tank pressure decreases to 300 psig, however, the spring pressure allows the valve to close. At this point air ceases to flow from the tank, and the diver must manually open the valve by pulling a valve lever. When pulled, this lever pulls the valve away from the seat, allowing air to flow to the diver. When used, a J valve must be in the up position at the beginning of the dive, and once pulled, the diver should surface. The J valve must be in the down position to be filled (see Figure 51).

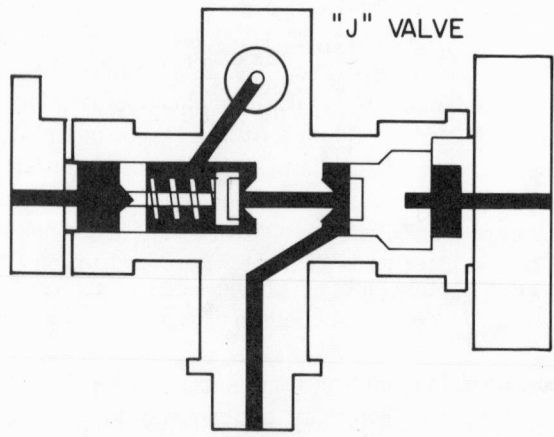

Fig. 51. Schematic of J valve.

The diver using a J valve should periodically check to be sure he has not accidentally bumped the lever down. He must also remember that if he travels away from the dive platform until he pulls his reserve, he has used approximately 2,000 psig traveling one way and it is not likely that he can return on 300 psig. It is therefore recommended that J valves only be used as backup mechanisms to submersible air pressure gauges. Many divers prefer to use a K valve and a submersible air pressure gauge.

For many forms of diving longer bottom times are desirable; thus, double tanks are used. When selecting a double-tank setup a diver must consider which type of double manifold he should use. The permanent manifold is the most popular and has proven to be quite safe. In this system the tanks are connected to each other and one regulator outlet is used.

A better system is one in which the tanks are connected by means of a permanent manifold that has two regulator outlets. In this ideal manifold either regulator can be shut off in the event of a malfunction, and the air supply will remain common to the one regulator. This system is also good for buddy breathing purposes and is already in common use in Europe.

Temporary yokes are frequently used for connecting two single tanks. The disadvantage of this system is that it requires perfect alignment of the tank valves. There is also a tendency to blow O rings when the yoke is bumped. Another method is to use two single tanks with a regulator on each tank. This method causes more damage to the regulator and can be disastrous to the diver. Usually the regulator that is not being used is being dragged through sand, silt, and trash. This causes internal damage to the regulator. The disaster occurs when the diver finishes the first tank, switches to the second, and the regulator malfunctions (see Figure 34 for double-tank setups and Chapter 7 for further discussion of tanks).

Care and maintenance of tanks includes rinsing with freshwater, storing with air in the tanks, and routine maintenance (VIP's, hydrostatings, etc.). Tanks being transported should be secured in a manner that prevents them from rolling around. Back packs or harnesses are used to carry the tanks and to attach them to the diver.

Closed- and Semiclosed-Circuit Scuba

Closed- and semiclosed-circuit scuba have the advantages of no air bubbles and prolonged durations. The advantage of no air bubbles is utilized both for military purposes and for behavioral studies of reef fish.

Closed-circuit oxygen rebreathers are used in water shallower than 25 feet. These systems come in two types, pendulum and recirculating (see Figure 52).

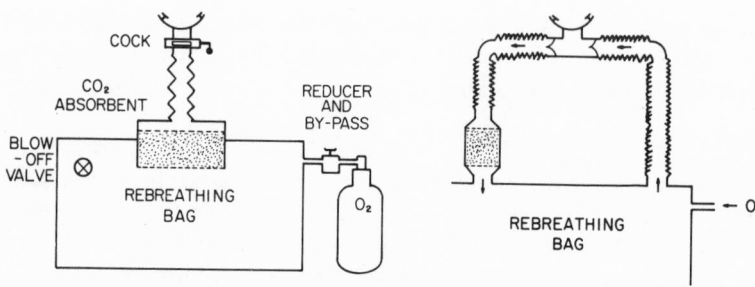

Fig. 52. Two types of closed-circuit rebreathers.
Left, pendulum breathing; *right,* recirculating.

The pendulum unit has the carbon dioxide absorbent so that the diver's gas is filtered on both inhalation and exhalation. This unit is more efficient than the recirculator but also has greater breathing resistance. A recirculating unit utilizes check valves, and the gas is filtered only on exhalation.

Semiclosed rebreathers are similar to closed-circuit rebreathers except a portion of the gas is vented. This system is used with mixed gases. Recent units feature electronic controls (see Figure 53).

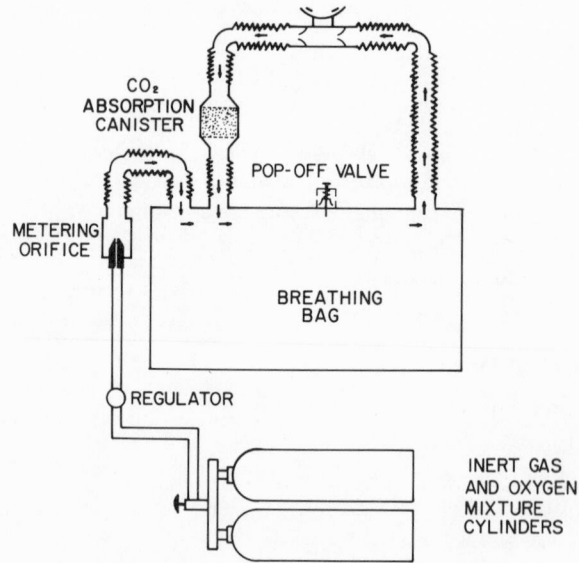

Fig. 53. Semiclosed-circuit rebreathers.

Although these units have many advantages, they are primarily used in conjunction with deep, lockout or saturation dives. Disadvantages of the units are expense and maintenance.

Surface-Supplied Equipment

A surface-supplied system is composed of an air supply (compressor), air hose, and either a helmet, a full face mask, or a demand regulator. These units afford less mobility than scuba but are preferred for working dives that do not require swimming great distances (see Figure 54).

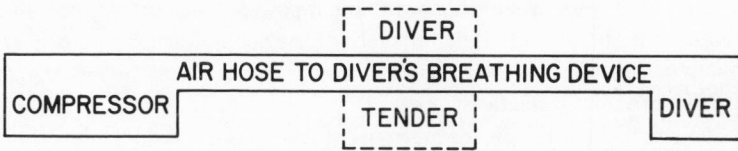

Fig. 54. Surface-supplied system.

Hard hat diving is used for heavy work or using gas. These systems relieve the diver of having to worry about his air supply, et cetera. The buddy in a surface-supplied system is a surface tender. In addition, this system has communications and a diver can be pulled to the surface should something happen.

Many projects using scuba could probably be more productive using Hookah (surface supplied with a demand regulator second stage), thus removing the weight and bulk of a tank.

Other Diver Support Equipment

The systems discussed so far have been the personal life support systems of the diver. For this equipment to function and to protect the diver, several other pieces of equipment are needed. These include boats, submersibles, diver transport units (scooters), habitats, compressors, and decompression chambers.

Compressors come in two basic types, low pressure and high pressure. Low-pressure compressors are used for supplying surface-supplied systems and decompression chambers. High-pressure compressors are used to charge scuba tanks. A compressor may be driven by either a gas or electric motor. When using gas or diesel fuel, care should be taken to isolate the compressor intake from engine exhaust. All compressors should incorporate a filter system for removing impurities. The filter material must be changed periodically. The accumulators and moisture trap must be bled at

15- to 30-minute intervals, and compressors should not be left unattended while in operation.

Decompression chambers are used to treat diving diseases. These units are high-pressure cylinders that have an input and exhaust valve system. Gauges are used to read the pressure or depth of the chamber. Special care must be taken to ventilate the chamber periodically. Most chambers are designed so that oxygen can be used when making treatment runs. As a result, the chamber cleanliness level has to be compatible for a high-pressure oxygen environment. No oil-based lubricants can be used in a chamber nor can people with oily clothing be allowed inside the chamber. Chambers are also fitted with both sound-powered and battery-powered communication systems. It is imperative that people operating chambers be trained in operating their specific chamber and that they be thoroughly familiar with safety practices.

The selection of the diver's life support system is a very individual thing and is dependent upon the type of dive to be performed. The type of equipment used and its care is a direct reflection of the diver's respect for himself and his buddy. Good equipment is like having a good insurance policy, only this policy protects you from something happening instead of taking care of you after it has happened.

Review questions for chapter 9

1. Concerning air compressor systems:
   (a) Give a short explanation of how a compressor functions to produce the quality and pressure of air used in scuba tanks.
   (b) What are some of the major concerns or problems that can be associated with faulty compressors?
2. Given the following tank markings:
   DOT 2250 3AA
   5 − 70 +
   (a) What does DOT mean?
   (b) What does 2250 mean?
   (c) What does 3AA mean?
   (d) What does 5 − 70 mean?
   (e) What does the + after 5 − 70 mean?
   (f) If SP were substituted for 3AA, what would that signify?
3. Your regulator continually feeds you a heavy mist of water. The problem most likely is_____
   or _____
4. Your regulator begins to free flow immediately upon turning it on.

The trouble is most likely in the _____ stage. If there were a slight delay and then a free flow, you would suspect the free flow to be in the _____ stage.

5. You have just put your tank on and you notice that when you inhale the seavue gauge drops from 2,000 psig to 1,000 psig. On exhalation, the seavue returns to 2,000 psig. This problem is one of human error and is most likely _____
   The effect of this problem at depth would be _____
   of air.

6. Draw a single-hose regulator with a standard diaphragm first stage and a tilt valve second stage.

7. Draw a flow-into piston first stage with a downstream second stage.

8. Draw a balanced piston first stage.

9. Draw a balanced diaphragm first stage.

10. Draw a double-hose single-stage regulator.

11. Draw a double-hose two-stage regulator.

12. A tank that is rated at 2,250 psig would be hydrostatically tested to _____ psig.

13. Explain the desirable characteristics of a buoyancy compensator.

14. Why are the following pieces of equipment mandatory for safe diving?
    (a) watch
    (b) depth gauge
    (c) buoyancy compensator

15. Give one reason for ventilating a decompression chamber.

16. Explain the principles of a wet suit and how you would select one.

17. Draw a recirculating rebreather.

18. What is the difference between a pendulum and recirculating rebreather?

19. Where is the safety blowoff disk located on most tank valves? Why?

20. Empty scuba tanks should be stored with some pressure in them to prevent
    (a) moisture from entering
    (b) carbon monoxide from entering
    (c) oxygen from entering
    (d) drying out

21. On a standard scuba tank, the air reserve usually retains about
    (a) 100 psi
    (b) 300 psi
    (c) 500 psi
    (d) 600 psi

22. The lens in a face plate should be
    (a) ordinary glass
    (b) plastic
    (c) tinted plastic
    (d) shatterproof glass
23. If breathing from your regulator becomes difficult after diving for some time, you would suspect that
    (a) the hose was plugged
    (b) the reserve was stuck
    (c) you had gone too deep
    (d) you are low on air
24. The diver's flag on a float indicates
    (a) divers are down and have the right-of-way over boatmen
    (b) divers are down and boats should keep clear of the area
    (c) the area is reserved for skin and scuba divers
    (d) the float is owned by a skin or scuba diver
25. The first piece of equipment ditched in an emergency or when in trouble is the
    (a) tank
    (b) weight belt
    (c) mask
    (d) safety vest
26. The most important thing to remember about your weight belt is that it should
    (a) weight you to neutral buoyancy
    (b) have weights at sides so they will not be under tank
    (c) be capable of release with one jerk of the hand and fall free
    (d) weight you to slightly positive buoyancy with full breath
27. The most important part of a life support system is
    (a) a thinking diver
    (b) an octopus system
    (c) a good buddy
    (d) a trained diver

10

RSMAS Diving Programs

Diving is an excellent research tool that opens up many new and exciting areas for study. It is a serious tool, however, and mistakes can result in accidents and even fatalities. The program of the Rosenstiel School of Marine and Atmospheric Science (RSMAS) is based on a philosophy of safety first and research second. This is not an unfair compromise, because in most instances the productivity of a diving project is directly related to the safety practices followed. The entire program depends on each individual accepting and enforcing his responsibilities as a diver.

It is hoped that through proper training and the use of common sense divers will enforce "good everyday diving habits" beyond the scope of any rules and regulations. In the various diver training programs, emphasis is placed on the diver's common sense and individual responsibilities as well as on the development of skill and technique.

The diving and training programs of the Rosenstiel School of Marine and Atmospheric Science are based on the following system of diver qualification levels (see also Figure 55).

Shallow Water Diver, 30-foot Qualification

Divers who possess a nationally recognized diving certification card and a log of three dives are classified as shallow water divers. They are authorized to dive to depths of 30 feet provided they are supervised by a research diver, category A (RDA).

Intermediate Diver, 60-foot Qualification

Classified as intermediate divers are those who have completed the research diver, category A program or those certified as advanced divers through national programs. Divers in this category are authorized to dive to depths of 60 feet provided they are supervised by an RDA. Upon

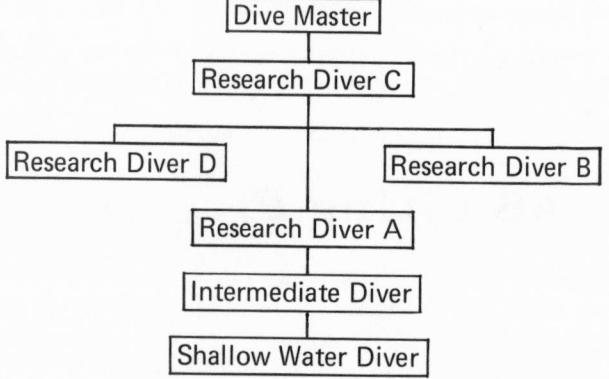

Fig. 55. Levels in diving proficiency.

logging 20 dives, an intermediate diver who has completed all qualifications for research diver, category A may be advanced to that level.

Research Diver, Category A (RDA), 90-foot Qualification

A diver who has completed the RDA training program and logged 20 dives may be classified as a research diver, category A. He is then authorized to dive to a maximum depth of 90 feet on no decompression dives.

The RDA program is an extensive program designed to instill a thorough knowledge of diving physics, diving physiology, oxygen, inert gases, decompression illness, decompression techniques, principles of safe diving, and life support equipment. Certification in basic Red Cross First Aid, Cardiopulmonary Resuscitation, and Senior Lifesaving is a part of the program, and all basic skills in skin and scuba diving, including navigation, are covered in the 100-hour course.

Research Diver, Category B, 180-foot Qualification

To qualify as a research diver, category B, a diver must have a log of 55 dives, 5 of which must be dives to 180 feet with a dive master; he must complete a course of approximately 30 hours duration, including both 180-foot chamber and open water dives; and he must be familiar with the operation of decompression chambers and compressors.

Research Diver, Category C, 200-foot Qualification

To qualify as a research diver, category C, a diver must have a log of 75 dives, including at least 15 dives between 100 and 180 feet.

Research Diver, Category D, Submarine Caves

To qualify as a research diver, category D, a diver must have a log of 80 dives with at least 5 dives to 180 feet and a minimum of 10 night dives.

Dive Master, 240-foot Qualification and Supervisory Rating

The title of dive master is awarded to those individuals with a log of 100 dives who demonstrate the maturity and good judgment necessary to supervise diving operations in a safe, efficient manner. It is the responsibility of the dive master to enforce safety rules and regulations and to maintain safe diving operations. He will report all violations of good diving practices or regulations to the diving officer. A dive master negligent in these responsibilities will lose his qualification.

The diving officer may waive the RDA qualification course for experienced divers who:

1. Pass a pool test on basic skills.
2. Complete a navigation test.
3. Pass a written theory test emphasizing diving theory.
4. Have certification in basic first aid and senior lifesaving.
5. Perform five evaluation dives with a dive master.

The course may also be waived for divers with certification through the U.S. Navy Underwater Swimmers School, the Scripps Institution of Oceanography, the University of Michigan, Florida SITS program, and programs equal to RSMAS and the National Association of Underwater Instructors (NAUI) or YMCA instructors.

A visiting scientist or consultant will be allowed to dive with an RDA diver or under the supervision of a dive master up to the equivalent category of the visiting scientist's dive rating.

To maintain dive status, a diver must

1. Log at least one dive every three months.
2. Pass a physical examination for divers once a year.
3. Adhere to rules and regulations.
4. Maintain a dive log.

Outline of RSMAS Diver Qualification Programs

Research Diver A Qualification Program

RDA course text: *Practical Diving—Medical Aspects of Sport Diving.* American Red Cross course books: *Basic First Aid* and *Life Saving and Water Safety Today.*

Day 1

Morning

8:00-8:50	Course orientation and objectives
9:00-10:15	Discussion of basic equipment
10:15	Break for lunch and obtaining personal equipment

Afternoon

1:00-1:50	Water safety
2:00-2:50	Psychological aspects of diving
3:00-4:20	Physics
4:30-5:20	Physiology

Day 2

Morning

8:00-Noon	Pool (swim qualifications, lifesaving skills)

Afternoon

1:00-2:20	Barotrauma
2:30-3:10	Oxygen poisoning
3:20-4:00	Inert gas narcosis
4:10-5:00	Breath-hold diving (free-diving) techniques

Day 3

Morning

8:00-Noon	Pool (free-diving skills, lifesaving)

Afternoon

1:00-2:50	Buoyancy control, body positioning, and techniques
3:00-5:00	Specialized diving environments

Day 4

Morning

8:00-Noon	Pool (lifesaving, free diving, introduction to scuba)

Afternoon

1:00-2:50	Decompression sickness
3:00-5:00	Introduction to dive tables

Day 5

Morning

8:00-Noon	Pool (lifesaving, scuba skills)

Afternoon

1:00-1:30	Spot written quiz
1:30-1:50	Review of quiz
2:00-3:50	Dive tables
4:00-5:00	Navigation

Day 6

Morning

8:00-Noon	Pool (scuba skills, lifesaving)

Afternoon
1:00-1:50	Navigation drill on land
2:00-2:50	Accident management and prevention
3:00-5:00	Scuba mechanics

Day 7

Morning
8:00-Noon	Pool (scuba skills)

Afternoon
1:00-5:00	First aid

Day 8

Morning
8:00-Noon	Pool (practical examination)

Afternoon
1:00-1:50	Familiarization with compressors and decompression chamber
2:00-3:00	Small-boat handling

Days 9 and 10
8:00-8:50	Load dive gear on board ship for open water, check out dives
9:00	Depart RSMAS
9:30-Noon	Written examination
1:00 P.M.	Arrive at dive site, commence diving (six dives minimum including one night dive)

Research Diver B Qualification Program

Texts: *Practical Diving, U.S. Navy Manuals, Research Dive Manual*

Day 1

Morning
9:00-10:50	Review of medical aspects of diving
11:00-12:00	General principles of operation of decompression chambers

Afternoon
1:00-2:50	Introduction to operation of decompression chambers
3:00-5:00	Chamber dive to 150 feet (students operate chamber)

Day 2

Morning
9:00-Noon	Pool (scuba skills, pool examination)

Afternoon
1:00-1:50	Treatment tables and selection of tables
2:00-5:00	Chamber dives to 180 feet (students operate chamber)

Day 3

Morning
9:00-Noon	Open water dive to 150 feet

Afternoon
1:00-5:00.   Chamber dive to 150 feet, oxygen decompression (students operate chamber)

Day 4
Morning
9:00-Noon   Open water dive to 180 feet
Afternoon
1:00-5:00   Chamber dive to 120 feet (students operate chamber)

Day 5
Morning
9:00-Noon   Open water dive to 180 feet
Afternoon   Written examination covering all phases of diving

Research Diver C Qualification Program

Texts: *Practical Diving, N.O.A.A. Dive Manual*

Day 1
Morning
9:00-Noon   Review of decompression techniques
Afternoon
1:00-5:00   Chamber dive to 200 feet (students operate chamber)

Day 2
Morning
9:00-Noon   200-foot dive, open water
Afternoon
1:00-5:00   First aid and management of diving accidents

Day 3
Morning
9:00-Noon   200-foot dive
Afternoon
1:00-5:00   Chamber operation

Research Diver D Qualification Program

Text: *Safe Cave Diving*

Day 1
Morning
9:00-Noon   Pool qualification examination
Afternoon
1:00-2:15   Cave environment
2:25-2:50   History of cave diving
3:00-5:00   Philosophy and psychological aspects of cave diving

Day 2
9:00-9:50   Cave diving techniques

10:00-10:50	Body positioning and buoyancy control
11:00-11:50	Line technique
Afternoon	
1:00-5:00	Pool (technique and skill development)

Day 3

Morning

9:00-Noon	Pool (technique and skill development)
Afternoon	
1:00-1:50	Planning a cave dive
2:00-2:50	Knots and lines
3:00-3:50	Maintenance of cave diving equipment

Days 4 through 7

	Field Trip
Dive No. 1.	Introductory dive, single tank
Dive No. 2.	Current dive, buddy breathe on octopus while exiting cave
Dive No. 3.	Students use reel
Dive No. 4.	Students use reel
Dive No. 5.	Develop a map and perform ecology survey
Dive No. 6.	Develop a map and perform ecology survey
Dive No. 7.	Introduction to permanent lines
Dive No. 8.	Utilization of navigation aids and offshoot lines

Day 8

Morning

9:00-Noon	Written examination

Dive Master Qualification Program

Texts: *Practical Diving, NAUI Dive Master Notes*

Day 1

Morning

9:00-9:50	Goals and objectives of the dive master program and assignment of student dive papers
10:00-10:50	Responsibilities of a dive master
11:00-11:50	Supervision of diving projects
Afternoon	
1:00-1:50	Review of treatment principles
2:00-5:00	Operation of decompression chamber (simulated treatment runs)

Day 2

8:00 A.M.	
5:00 P.M.	Advanced first aid and emergency medical data collection

Day 3

Morning

9:00-Noon	Small-boat handling and water safety
Afternoon	
1:00-2:50	Papers presented (these are the papers assigned on the first day)
3:00-5:00	Written examination

In addition to the preceding, all dive masters must assist with the pool training sessions in one RDA program. This experience aids the dive master in developing an understanding and awareness of the novice diver.

In conclusion, the major emphasis of this diver training program is on safety and the application of common sense. Perhaps one of the greatest assets to safety is a realistic buddy system. A buddy system is not two divers entering and exiting the water together; a buddy system is a team of divers functioning as one unit, each being continually aware of his buddy at all times. The buddy can prevent critical incidents and can assist in overcoming problems that may be encountered on a dive. The buddy cannot breathe or make prolonged swims for someone else. Divers should practice survival buddymanship until it is second nature. This means avoiding panic situations. Distances between buddies should not exceed one-half the range of visibility. In clear water the maximum safe distance between buddies is one-half of the distance a buddy can swim without needing air.

Selected Bibliography

Bennett, P. G. 1966. *The aetiology of compressed air intoxication and inert gas narcosis.* Oxford: Pergamon Press.

Bennett, P. B., and Elliott, D. H., eds. 1969. *The physiology and medicine of diving and compressed air work.* Baltimore: Williams & Wilkins.

Chance, B., Jamieson, E., and E. Williamson. 1966. Control of the oxidation-reduction state of reduced pyridine nucleotides in vivo and in vitro by hyperbaric oxygen. In *Proceedings of the Third International Conference on Hyperbaric Medicine,* edited by I. W. Brown and B. G. Cox. Washington, D.C.: National Academy of Sciences, National Research Council.

Dueker, C. L. 1970. *Medical aspects of sport diving.* Cranbury, N.J.: A.S. Barnes & Co.

Goff, Loyal G., ed. 1955. *Underwater physiology symposium.* Proceedings of the First Underwater Physiology Symposium, Jan. 10-11, 1955. Washington, D.C.: National Academy of Sciences, publication 377.

Lambertsen, C. J., ed. 1967. *Proceedings of the Third Symposium on Underwater Physiology.* Baltimore Williams & Wilkins.

Lambertsen, C. J., ed. 1971. *Underwater physiology.* New York: Academic Press.

Lambertsen, C. J., and Greenbaum, L. J., eds. 1963. *Symposium on underwater physiology.* Proceedings of the Second Symposium on Underwater Physiology, Feb. 25-26, 1963. Washington, D.C.: National Academy of Sciences, Mine Advisory Committee, publication 1181.

Miles, S. 1966. *Underwater medicine.* London: Staples Press.

Mount, Tom. *Safe cave diving.* Gainesville, Fla.: National Association for Cave Diving.

Council for National Cooperation in Aquatics. 1974. *New science of skin and scuba.* 4th edition. New York: Association Press.

Philp, R. B. 1967. Decompression sickness in experimental animals. In *Symposium on underwater physiology.* Baltimore: Williams & Wilkins.

Smith, R. 1973. Stress in cave diving. In *Safe cave diving,* edited by Tom Mount. Gainesville, Fla.: National Association for Cave Diving.

Sommers, Lee. 1972. *Research divers manual.* Ann Arbor: University of Michigan, Seagrant Program.

Tank facts. 1973. Colton, Calif.: National Association of Underwater Instructors.

U.S. Navy diving manual. 1970. Washington, D.C.: U.S. Government Printing Office.

Appendix A:

University of Miami RSMAS Scuba Qualification Application

Name .... RSMAS Phone ext. ....

Address .... Division ....

Date .... Age .... Sex .... (circle) Student .... Employee ....

Is diving a part of your research or job? ....

Purpose for diving (be specific) ....

....

....
    Signature   Signature of Division Chairman   Date

Approved   Disapproved   Signature and Date

....   Faculty Advisor or Supervisor ....

....   Dean of Student Affairs ....

....   Diving Officer ....

....   Student Health Center M. D. ....

Diving physical to be charged to ....

Evaluation

Written exam .... Pool test ....

Open water proficiency (5 - 10 - 6 needed for passing)

Dive

	1	2	3	4	5	6
Planning	......	......	......	......	......	......
Buoyancy control	......	......	......	......	......	......
Relaxation	......	......	......	......	......	......
Buddymanship	......	......	......	......	......	......
Awareness	......	......	......	......	......	......
Navigation	......	......	......	......	......	......
Average	......	......	......	......	......	......
Instructor's initial	......	......	......	......	......	......

Certified .... Not Certified .... D. O.

Appendix B:

RSMAS Sample Written Examinations

Sample Examination 1: Research Diver Category A

1. Air is composed of _____% nitrogen. At the surface the PO_2 is ____ and the percentage of N_2 in the gas at this depth is _____.

2. A diver weighs 169 pounds and displaces 2 2/3 cubic feet. Will the diver sink or float in freshwater? In saltwater?

3. Boyle's Law explains the relationship in changes of ____ and _____. This is a foundation for understanding
    (a) oxygen poisoning and inert gas narcosis
    (b) decompression sickness
    (c) air embolism and squeezes
    (d) hypoglycemia

4. Match the following: (a) Solubility
    __ Dalton's Law   (b) Buoyancy
    __ Henry's Law   (c) Partial pressures
    __ Pascal's Principle   (d) Gas diffusion
    __ Archimedes' Principle (e) Pressure transmitted in liquid
                             (f) Temperature versus volume changes

5. A double tank unit will last a diver 90 minutes at 33 feet. How long will the same unit last the diver at 165 feet?

6. Draw a diagram showing the stimulation and production of respiration.

7. The central nervous system consists of
    (a) brain and spinal cord
    (b) cranial and spinal nerves
    (c) nerves of the feet and hands
    (d) none of the above

8. List the six steps of respiration and indicate which steps make up internal respiration.

9. The two systems that make up the circulatory system are the
    (a) arterial and capillary
    (b) veins and capillary
    (c) pulmonary and arterial
    (d) pulmonary and systemic

10. Explain and draw a diagram expressing why it is important to breathe slowly and deeply when using scuba.

11. Intentional hyperventilation is
    (a) overbreathing to increase PO_2
    (b) overbreathing to numb the chemoreceptors
    (c) overbreathing to take advantage of a denser gas
    (d) overbreathing to blow off CO_2

12. Circle factors affecting unintentional hyperventilation:
    (a) emotional stress
    (b) anxiety
    (c) relaxation
    (d) overworking

Barotrauma

13. List three ways of equalizing pressure on the ears and sinuses during descent.

14. Give two symptoms of each of the following:
    (a) air embolism
    (b) pneumothorax
    (c) mediastinal emphysema

15. If a scuba diver surfaces, exhales and immediately becomes unconscious, what would you most likely suspect his problem to be? What would be your immediate reaction and first aid? What is the treatment for this diving accident? How could the above accident have been prevented?

16. Draw and label the sinuses.

Oxygen poisoning and inert gas narcosis

17. Chronic oxygen poisoning is more common among (saturation, or deep, short bounce dives). This condition can be avoided by
    (a) using gas mixture containing gases less dense than air containing gases less dense than air
    (b) reducing the percentage of oxygen in the mixture, when working at greater depths
    (c) using drugs to avoid congestion by oxygen
    (d) none of the above

18. List three symptoms of acute oxygen poisoning.

19. Explain the Meyer-Overton hypothesis.

20. Which of the following is most affected by inert gas narcosis?
    (a) Manual skill
    (b) Muscle control
    (c) Mental function
    (d) Sexual performance

21. Give at least three contributory factors to narcosis.

Decompression sickness

22. It is recommended that divers perform moderate exercise during decompression in order to stimulate better circulation, thereby reducing the possibility of developing decompression sickness. (True or false)

23. Nitrogen is five times as soluble in fat as in aqueous tissue, therefore more nitrogen will dissolve in fat; however, due to its high solubility in fat, nitrogen will also "bleed off" from fat tissues faster, thereby causing a fat person to be less susceptible to decompression sickness. (True or false)

24. List three protective steps a diver should take to aid in preventing decompression sickness.

25. Give two symptoms of decompression sickness affecting the following areas:
    (a) skeletal system
    (b) respiratory system
    (c) nervous system
    (d) circulatory system

26. In developing a theory for safely decompressing divers, Haldane made three basic determinations. What were they?

27. What is the treatment for decompression sickness?

28. After a no decompression dive, a minimum of _____ hours should pass prior to flying. After a decompression dive, the diver should remain on the surface _____ hours.

Plan the following dives

29. 60 feet 50 minutes stops _____ Group _____
60 feet _____ maximum bottom time with no decompression Group _____

30. 70 feet 40 minutes stops _____ Group _____
surface interval 2 hours Group _____
80 feet 35 minutes stops _____ Group _____
surface interval 4 hours Group _____
60 feet _____ maximum bottom time with no decompression Group _____

31. 90 feet 20 minutes stops. _____ Group _____
minimum surface interval _____ Group _____
60 feet 24 minutes without a need to decompress Group _____

32. 30 feet   125 minutes stops _____Group _____
2 hours surface interval _____Group _____
20 feet   160 minutes _____ Group _____
1.5 hours surface interval _____Group _____
60 feet   60 minutes stops _____ Group _____

33. 90 feet   30 minutes stops _____Group _____
5 minute surface interval _____ Group _____
90 feet   30 minutes stops _____Group _____

34. 100 feet 30 minutes, and the diver accidently surfaces; wha would be his hew decompression schedule?

35. 210 feet 15 minutes stops _____ Group _____
minimum surface interval _____
210 feet   30 minutes stops _____

36. The ideal common sense versus physical ability ratio is
    (a) 50:50
    (b) 40:60
    (c) 70:30
    (d) 60:40

37. List four sources of stress to which a diver is subjected.

38. A safe diving philosophy includes
    (a) self-honesty, assumption of responsibilities, defensive buddy concept, and dive planning
    (b) self-honesty, selectivity, and always diving up to one's own capacity
    (c) dive planning, diving the plan, and responding to challenge
    (d) incorporating the defensive buddy system, developing total self-confidence so that the diver can cope with virtually any situation that may occur

39. Emotional fitness of a diver includes the following three factors:
    (a) awareness, selectivity, and physical competence
    (b) relaxation, self-honesty, and good watermanship
    (c) common sense, maturity, and self-discipline
    (d) motivation, relaxation, and physical fitness

40. When faced with a stressful situation the diver should
    (a) react quickly as any delay may worsen the situation
    (b) worry about the situation before him
    (c) allow the more experienced diver to make all decisions
    (d) stop, think, react

41. Panic is
    (a) a normal flight reaction

    (b) the point when mental consciousness losses control over physical response

    (c) a normal fight reaction

    (d) both b and c

42. Panic may be prevented through self-discipline, anticipation, over-training, and determination of the exact situation. (True or false)

43. What are the three major responsibilities of a diver?

44. The four primary points of a good dive plan are

    (a) determining the air cutoff point, selecting the correct technique, ensuring the dive plan is adhered to strictly, and appointing the most experienced diver as dive master.

    (b) ensuring each diver is properly equipped, training in specialized technique, determining that all air can be used so that none is wasted by returning partially filled tanks to the surface, and planning the dive around the least experienced diver.

    (c) determining that each diver understands the group is to surface when the first diver hits reverse or 300 psig, selecting correct technique, establishing a maximum depth and bottom time, and setting the maximum number of divers on the dive.

    (d) information gathering, group planning, individual planning, and self-preparation.

Physical performance and different diving environments

45. In order to develop a reasonable air-used versus distance-traveled ratio, one must maintain proper trim and employ correct swim techniques. (True or false)

46. What is the most practical method to calculate air used on a given dive? When making a comparison betwen divers using different tank volumes

    (a) determine psig used per minute

    (b) determine cubic footage used per minute

    (c) determine total psig used on dive

    (d) determine total cubic footage used on dive

47. When establishing the desired swim speed a balance must be made between

    (a) average speed and air consumption

    (b) maximum speed and air consumption

    (c) average speed and fatigue

48. What are three causes of currents?

49. To escape from a rip current
    (a) swim parallel to the beach
    (b) swim toward the shore
    (c) swim away from the shore
    (d) ride the current out and wait for help

50. List the precautions you would take when making a night dive.

51. List three reasons why cave diving is considered hazardous.

Equipment

52. When should a weight belt be put on? When removed?

53. When your regulator continually feeds you a fine mist of water, what are the two most likely problems?

54. Draw a diagram of a balanced-piston first-stage regulator with a downstream second stage.

55. Draw a standard diaphragm first-stage regulator with a tilt valve second stage.

56. Why are the following pieces of equipment mandatory for safe diving?
    (a) Watch
    (b) Depth gauge
    (c) Buoyancy compensator
    (d) Submersible dive tables

57. How often should tanks be hydrostated? How often is it recommended that they be visually inspected?

58. Draw a closed-circuit rebreather.

59. Explain the following tank markings.
    (a) DOT
    (b) 2250
    (c) 3AA
    (d) SP on aluminum tanks
    (e) 5 − 74 +

60. You have just put your tank on and you notice that when you inhale, the seavue gauge drops from 2,000 psig to 500 psig. On exhalation the gauge returns to 2,000 psig. The most likely problem is
    (a) sticking needle on seavue gauge
    (b) air not turned on fully
    (c) clogged high-pressure port on the first stage of the regulator

61. The most important part of a life support system is
    (a) an octopus system
    (b) a regulator featuring low-inhalation resistance, low-exhalation resistance, and adequate volume

(c) a good buddy
(d) a logical, thinking diver

Sample Examination 2: Research Diver Category D

History

1. Lirou Cave was the site of the first
   (a) complete cave map
   (b) cave diving fatality
   (c) cave dive
   (d) cave diving seminar
2. NACD was organized in
   (a) 1945
   (b) 1966
   (c) 1969
   (d) 1971
3. The first map of a water-filled cave was that of
   (a) Radium Springs
   (b) Manatee Spring
   (c) Wakulla Spring
   (d) Devil's Hole

Environment

4. What are the four types of caves?
5. Which of the following is not a type of sedentary rock in which solution usually occurs?
   (a) Shale
   (b) Dolomite
   (c) Gypsum
   (d) Limestone
6. The major structural control for most cavern development in Florida is
   (a) faults
   (b) breakdown
   (c) bedding planes
   (d) joints or fractures
   (e) folding
7. The general natural hazards (found in all caves) of underwater caves are water, darkness, and
   (a) silt
   (b) panicked divers
   (c) the ceiling of the cave

(d) mazes

(e) scadgetts

8. Four physical pecularities of underwater caves that can be hazardous are very large caves, deep caves mazes, and

(a) panicked divers

(b) narcosis

(c) rip tides

(d) restrictions

(e) sharks

9. List three categories of silt.

10. List four parts of a spring.

11. Two primary considerations to be made in regard to current are

(a) depth of water, restrictions

(b) direction and velocity

(c) water clarity and time of day

(d) none of the above

Psychological Aspects of Cave Diving

12. Which of the following is the ideal ratio of common sense to physical ability?

(a) 50:50

(b) 40:60

(c) 70:30

(d) 60:40

13. List four sources of stress to which a cave diver is subjected.

14. Which of the following are included in a safe diving philosophy?

(a) Self-honesty, assumption of responsibilities, defensive buddy concept, and dive planning.

(b) Self-honesty, selectivity, and always diving up to one's own capacity.

(c) Dive planning, diving the plan, and responding to challenge.

(d) Incorporating the defensive buddy system, developing total self-confidence so that the diver can cope with virtually any situation that may occur.

15. Emotional fitness of a diver includes three factors which are

(a) awareness, selectivity, and physical competence

(b) relaxation, self-honesty, and good watermanship

(c) common sense, maturity, and self-discipline

(d) motivation, relaxation, and physical fitness

16. When faced with a stressful situation the diver should

(a) react quickly as any delay may worsen the situation

(b) worry about the situation before him

(c) allow the more experienced diver to make all decisions

(d) stop, think, react

17. Panic is
    (a) a normal flight reaction
    (b) the point when mental consciousness loses control over physical response
    (c) a normal fight reaction
    (d) both b and c

18. Panic may be prevented through self-discipline, anticipation, over-raining, and determination of the exact situation. (True or false)

19. What are a diver's three major responsibilities?

20. The four primary points of a good dive plan are
    (a) determining the air cutoff point; selecting the correct technique; ensuring strict adherence to the dive plan; and appointing the most experienced diver as dive master.
    (b) ascertaining that each diver is properly equipped; training in specialized technique; determining that all air can be used so that none is wasted by returning partially filled tanks to the surface; and planning the dive around the least experienced diver.
    (c) determining that each diver understands the group is to surface when the first diver hits reserve or 300 psig; selecting correct technique; establishing a maximum depth and bottom time; and setting the maximum number of divers on the dive.
    (d) information gathering; group planning; individual planning; and self-preparation.

21. Circle the four most pertinent factors in developing a good philosophy for cave diving.
    (a) Good line technique
    (b) A working approach to dive planning
    (c) Assumption of responsibilities
    (d) Extreme self-confidence
    (e) Physical/mental relationship
    (f) Psychological adjustments

22. Match the following:
    (a) Buddy team   1. Earn respect and give respect
    (b) Dive plan   2. Two individuals diving together
    (c) Live and let live   3. Sets definite objectives
    (d) Self-honesty   4. Leave others alone and be left alone
       5. Establishes maximums
       6. A unit acting as one force

23. On a dive with a new buddy, you should dive up to your limitations and depend on him to establish his limits. (True or false)

Life Support Systems

24. List four specialized types of equipment for cave diving.
25. The three most important functions of a life support system are
    (a) comfort, fit, and preference
    (b) breathing mixture, easy inhalation, and adequate volume
    (c) adequate breathing mixture, proper buoyancy, and a propulsion mechanism
    (d) low inhalation resistance, a minimum of exhalation resistance, and high volume
26. Label the following double-tank setups in order of preference.
    (a) Two separate systems
    (b) Permanent manifold
    (c) Ideal manifold
    (d) Temporary yokes
27. What type of knife is suitable for use in cave diving?
28. Diving lights should be
    (a) water and pressure resistant
    (b) rugged and compact
    (c) dependable
    (d) all the above
29. The most important part of a life support system is
    (a) a thinking diver
    (b) an octopus system
    (c) a good buddy
    (d) a trained diver
30. List three desirable characteristics of a safety reel for cave diving.

Buoyancy Control

31. Circle factors that will cause changes in the diver's buoyancy during a dive.
    (a) Wet suit compression
    (b) Wet suit
    (c) Mask volume
    (d) Changes in air volume in tank
    (e) Light systems
    (f) Changes in depth
32. The buoyant state of the cave diver in full gear does not depend on
    (a) the diver's attitude with respect to the direction of the line
    (b) the amount of air in his compensator

(c) his depth

(d) the temperature of the water

33. Choose the incorrect statement.

(a) The drag force depends upon the speed and frontal area of the diver.

(b) The buoyant force always acts in the vertical.

(c) A motionless diver with horizontal trim has three forces acting on him.

(d) A diver buoyed positively must swim with a head down trim in order to maintain a constant swim depth.

34. A crotch strap is needed to prevent the buoyancy compensator from riding up on the neck. (True or false)

35. Explain the advantages of an automatic inflator attached to the buoyancy compensator.

36. Does the magnitude of the life force increase or decrease as the angle of attack increases?

37. Positive buoyancy will result in

(a) head up trim

(b) head down trim

(c) head and body level trim

(d) or will depend on the type of buoyancy compensator

38. In order to develop a reasonable ratio of air used to distance traveled, one must maintain proper trim and employ correct swim techniques. (True or false)

39. What is the most practical method to calculate air used on a given dive? When making comparisons between divers using different tank volumes the most practical method would be to

(a) determine the psig used per minute

(b) determine the cubic footage used per minute

(c) determine the total psig used on the dive

(d) determine the total cubic footage used on the dive

40. When establishing the desired swim speed, a balance must be made between

(a) average speed and air consumption

(b) maximum speed and air consumption

(c) average speed and fatigue

Technique

41. Three things must be analyzed prior to deciding on a given technique. They are

(a) cave configuration, life support system, and buddy

(b) current, silt, and bottom time

  (c) selection of proper technique, correct employment of the
       technique, and cave configuration
  (d) depth, bottom time, and air duration

42. Name four factors that should be taken into consideration when
selecting a technique to use in passing through a given cave configuration.

43. All good cave divers can dive most caves using only a couple of
techniques. (True or false and qualify your answer)

44. Pulling along with the arms usually is more efficient in terms of
air consumption than is kicking. (True or false)

Safety Lines

45. To maintain drag in order to run a taut line, the diver should
  (a) use a rubber drag on the reel drum.
  (b) allow the reel to free wheel and then stretch it at the points
       where he desires to make safety ties.
  (c) place his thumb or finger along the reel drum to act as drag.
  (d) turn periodically and reel the line tight.

46. Briefly state the responsibilities of the reel man.

47. The best knot for permanent installation using # 18-braided
nylon line is a
  (a) square knot
  (b) bowline with a backup knot
  (c) fisherman's knot
  (d) becket bend

48. What is the best knot to use when splicing lines of different sizes
together?

49. When tying a line to relieve strain one should use
  (a) two wraps
  (b) no wraps
  (c) three to five wraps
  (d) as many wraps as possible

50. On exiting a cave, the reel man's buddy has several major responsibilities. List three.

51. What are the four major responsibilities that must be considered
when installing a permanent line?

52. Lines tied within sight of surface light and extending a distance of
200 to 300 feet into popular caves are known as _____ lines.

53. Offshoot lines should have a gap of _____ feet from the
permanent line.
  (a) 40 to 50
  (b) 15 to 25

(c) 10 to 20

(d) 5 to 15

54. Why is education of the general public essential in terms of cave living?

(a) We, as cave diving instructors, want to recruit as many people as possible into our fast-growing sport.

(b) Better understanding by the public will lessen the possibility of access to springs and sinks being cut off.

(c) We want the landowners to see how wrong they were when they spoke disparagingly of cave divers.

(d) None of the above. (Please write the correct answer on the back of this page.)

55. Which of the following is not a goal of a cave diving course as taught by an NACD instructor?

(a) To train cave divers so well that all potential danger is completely eliminated.

(b) To teach the beginning cave diver the proper techniques that are essential to safe cave diving.

(c) To mold the thinking patterns of the beginning cave diver.

(d) To determine that the beginning cave diver is sincerely interested in cave diving per se.

Diving Physiology and Medicine

56. The central nervous system consists of

(a) the brain and spinal cord

(b) the cranial and spinal nerves

(c) the nerves of the feet and hands

(d) none of the above

57. List the six steps of respiration and indicate which steps make up internal respiration.

58. Explain why it is important to breathe slowly and deeply when using scuba. Draw a diagram to illustrate your answer.

59. Intentional hyperventilation is

(a) overbreathing to increase PO_2

(b) overbreathing to numb the chemoreceptors

(c) overbreathing to take advantage of a denser gas

(d) overbreathing to blow off CO_2

60. Circle factors affecting unintentional hyperventilation.

(a) Emotional stress

(b) Anxiety

(c) Relaxation

     (d) Overworking
61. Give two symptoms of each of the following.
     (a) Air embolism
     (b) Pneumothorax
     (c) Mediastinal emphysema
62. A scuba diver surfaces, exhales, and immediately becomes unconscious. What would you suspect his problem to be? What immediate first aid would you give? What treatment is correct for this diving accident? How is this type of accident prevented?
63. Is chronic O_2 poisoning more common after saturation dives or after deep, short bounce dives? This condition can be avoided by
     (a) using gas mixtures that contain gases that are less dense than air
     (b) reducing the percentage of oxygen in the mixture when working at greater depths
     (c) using drugs to avoid congestion caused by oxygen
     (d) none of the above
64. List three symptoms of acute oxygen poisoning.
65. Explain the Meyer-Overton hypothesis.
66. Which of the following is most affected by inert gas narcosis?
     (a) Manual skill
     (b) Muscle control
     (c) Mental function
     (d) Sexual performance
67. Give at least three contributory factors to narcosis.

Decompression Sickness

68. It is recommended that divers perform moderate exercise during decompression in order to stimulate better circulation, thereby reducing the possibility of developing decompression sickness. (True or false)
69. Nitrogen is five times as soluble in fat as in aqueous tissues; therefore more nitrogen will dissolve in fat. Due to its high solubility in fat, however, nitrogen will also "bleed off" from fat tissues faster; thereby causing a fat person to be less susceptible to decompression sickness. (True or false)
70. List three protective steps a diver should take to aid in preventing decompression sickness.
71. Give two symptoms of decompression sickness affecting the skeletal system.
72. Give two symptoms of decompression sickness affecting the respiratory system.

73. Give two symptoms of decompression sickness affecting the nervous system.

74. In developing a theory for safely decompressing divers, Haldane made three basic determinations. What were they?

75. What is the treatment for decompression sickness?

76. After a no decompression dive a minimum of _____ hours should pass prior to flying. After a decompression dive the diver should remain on the surface _____ hours.

Plan the following dives.

77. 60 feet 50 minutes stops _____ Group _____
Surface interval 4 hours   Group _____
60 feet _____ maximum bottom time without a need to decompress Group _____

78. 70 feet 40 minutes stops _____Group _____
Surface interval 2 hours Group _____
80 feet 35 minutes stops _____ Group _____
Surface interval 4 hours   Group _____
60 feet _____ maximum bottom time without a need to decompress Group _____

79. 90 feet 20 minutes stops _____ Group _____
Minimum surface interval _____Group _____
60 feet 24 minutes without a need to decompress   Group _____

80. 30 feet 125 minutes stops _____ Group _____
2 hours surface interval   Group _____
20 feet 160 minutes stops _____ Group _____
1.5 hours surface interval   Group _____
60 feet 60 minutes stops _____Group _____

81. 90 feet 30 minutes stops _____ Group _____
5 minute surface interval   Group _____
90 feet 30 minutes stops _____ Group _____

82. 100 feet 30 minutes, and the diver accidently surfaces. What would be his new decompression schedule? _____

Sample Written Examination 3

Physics

1. Boyle's Law best explains what three things?
    (a) Air embolism
    (b) Nitrogen narcosis
    (c) Oxygen toxicity
    (d) Ear squeeze

    (e) Lung squeeze

    (f) Hypercapnia

  2. List the three major constituents of air

  3. The partial pressure of O_2 at a depth of 61 feet is

    (a) 27.145 psi

    (b) 41.845 psi

    (c) 8.369 psi

    (d) 33.476 psi

    (e) 5.880 psi

  4. An air supply rated at 100 cubic feet at a pressure of 2,200 psig will last a diver breathing .5 cubic foot per minute, with only 1,800 psig in the tanks, how long at a depth of 132 feet?

    (a) 81.8 minutes

    (b) 50 minutes

    (c) 32.7 minutes

    (d) 44 minutes

  5. A tank is charged to 2,485 psig at a temperature of 60°C. What is the pressure when the air inside the tank has dropped to 40°F?

    (a) 2,235 psig

    (b) 3,000 psig

    (c) 1,800 psig

    (d) 1,945 psig

  6. Partial pressures are governed by _____ Law, while solubility is explained in _____ Law.

Physiology

  7. The three major systems in the body that man is most concerned with are _____ , _____ , and _____ .

  8. An average man's vital capacity ranges from:

    (a) 1 to 2 liters

    (b) 2 to 4 liters

    (c) 4 to 5 liters

    (d) 5 to 6 liters

  9. The greatest volume of air able to be moved in and out of the lungs in one breath:

    (a) respiratory cycle

    (b) vital capacity

    (c) respiratory rate

    (d) residual volume

  10. Air entering the lungs encounters the named parts in what order?

    (a) Alveoli, bronchial tubes, bronchioles

   (b) Bronchiole, bronchial tubes, alveoli
   (c) Bronchial tube, bronchiole, alveoli
   (d) Bronchiole, alveoli, bronchial tube
11. The substance that aids the blood in carrying oxygen is
   (a) the plasma
   (b) the serum
   (c) adrenalin
   (d) hemoglobin
12. Dead spaces associated with respiration are
   (a) ears, intestines, diaphragm
   (b) mouth, trachea, and bronchi
   (c) alveoli, pulmonary capillaries, tissues
13. The process of respiration includes
   (a) inhalation, alveolar exchange, chest expansion, N_2 exchange in tissues for energy
   (b) breathing, alveolar exchange, transportation of gases via circulatory system, use of CO_2 for heat production
   (c) breathing, alveolar exchange, transportation via circulatory system, capillary exchange, tissue exchange, and metabolism
14. Arrange the following to reflect the stimulation and production of respiration. Explain the process.
   (a) CO_2
   (b) Respiratory muscles
   (c) Muscular effort inhalation
   (d) Respiratory center

Barotrauma
15. Squeeze is the result of air pressure within a space being
   (a) less than external pressure
   (b) more than external pressure
   (c) equal to external pressure
   (d) equal to ambient pressure
16. Thoracic squeeze is
   (a) squeeze in the upper sinuses
   (b) supersaturated nitrogen in the tissues
   (c) compression of lungs below their residual volume
   (d) blockage of the carotid artery
17. Which symptom is not attributable to a type of squeeze?
   (a) Pain in a filled tooth
   (b) Bloodshot eyes
   (c) Blood in the mask

    (d) Welts under a wet suit

    (e) Pain in the throat

18. Which of the following is least likely to be a symptom of a ruptured eardrum?

    (a) Vertigo

    (b) Nasal bleeding

    (c) Nausea

    (d) Pain behind the eyes

    (e) Impaired hearing

19. Which of the following is least likely to be a symptom of sinus squeeze?

    (a) Pain behind the eyes

    (b) Vertigo

    (c) Nasal bleeding

    (d) Numbness of the upper teeth

    (e) Pain across the forehead

20. A pneumothorax is caused by

    (a) air around the heart

    (b) air under the skin

    (c) air in the bloodstream

    (d) air between the chest wall and lung

21. Air under the skin in the neck and shoulder areas is a symptom of

    (a) mediastinal emphysema

    (b) subcutaneous emphysema

    (c) pneumothorax

    (d) air embolism

22. Air in the tissues of the middle chest is called

    (a) air embolism

    (b) carotid sinus reflex

    (c) mediastinal emphysema

    (d) aeroembolism

23. An air embolism is caused by

    (a) staying too long at depth

    (b) cold water at depth

    (c) the expansion of trapped compressed air

    (d) the partial pressure of carbon dioxide

24. Give treatment for each of the following.

    (a) Air embolism

    (b) Ear squeeze

    (c) Pneumothorax

    (d) Lung squeeze

P₂, N₂, CO₂, and CO

25. At what depth does pure oxygen become toxic to a diver?
    (a) Below 25 feet
    (b) Below 60 feet
    (c) Below 100 feet
    (d) Below 300 feet
26. Nausea, muscular twitching, dizziness, disturbances of vision, convulsive seizure, etc., are some of the symptoms of
    (a) carbon dioxide poisoning
    (b) oxygen poisoning
    (c) bends
    (d) spontaneous pneumothorax
27. Oxygen poisoning is most commonly seen in the use of
    (a) scuba gear
    (b) rebreathing apparatus
    (c) hard-hat gear
    (d) skin diving gear
28. The greatest hazard of nitrogen narcosis is the
    (a) slowing of mental acitvity
    (b) slowing of reactions
    (c) diver's indifference to safety precautions
    (d) inability to do simple jobs
29. At what minimum depth can nitrogen narcosis usually become apparent?
    (a) 33 feet
    (b) 50 feet
    (c) 100 feet
    (d) 150 feet
    (e) 200 feet
30. Circle true statements concerning N_2 narcosis.
    (a) N_2 acts as a stimulant on the CNS
    (b) N_2 acts as a stimulant on the autonomic nervous system
    (c) N_2 acts as a depressant on the CNS
    (d) N_2 under pressure has an intoxicating effect on man
31. Which is not a symptom of CO toxicity?
    (a) Cherry red lips
    (b) Nausea
    (c) Blue fingernails
    (d) Dizziness
    (e) Headache
32. The respiratory quotient is the ratio between carbon dioxide out-

put and oxygen intake. Under normal conditions, the amount of carbon dioxide produced for every liter of oxygen consumed approximates

    (a) .5 liter

    (b) 1 liter

    (c) 1.5 liter

    (d) 2 liters

33. In the presence of CO poisoning, what are the signs that can be directly observed in an unconscious victim? Check correct answers.

    (a) Respiratory rate is increased.

    (b) Respiratory minute volume is increased.

    (c) Oxygen consumption is increased.

    (d) Cardiac rate is increased.

    (e) Lips and fingernails turn red.

    (f) Lips and fingernails turn blue.

34. Which is not a symptom of carbon dioxide excess?

    (a) Nausea

    (b) Headache

    (c) Bleeding from the nose

    (d) Dizziness

35. Oxygen usually comprises what percentage of air?

    (a) 5%

    (b) 12%

    (c) 21%

    (d) 49%

    (e) 100%

36. Unconsciousness can first be expected when the O_2 level is reduced to what partial pressure

    (a) 1.0 atm.

    (b) .20 atm.

    (c) .15 atm.

    (d) .10 atm.

    (e) .05 atm.

Decompression

37. The indirect cause of decompression sickness is

    (a) improper decompression

    (b) improper recompression

    (c) surfacing while holding your breath

    (d) going too deep, too long, with nitrogen in your gas mixture

38. A diver can, after deep diving, begin to show symptoms from the bends as long as _____ hours after leaving the water.

   (a) 6
   (b) 24
   (c) 12
   (d) 18

39. Which of the following statements is true about decompression sickness?

   (a) Decompression sickness involves joints only.
   (b) If left untreated, bends may progress to more serious manifestations of decompression sickness.
   (c) Bends pain is more serious than shortness of breath, chest pain, and dry cough.
   (d) Bends symptoms will always appear within 10 minutes after surfacing.
   (d) If a recompression chamber is not immediately available, begin treatment by recompressing in the water.

40. Which of the following is an important factor in producing decompression sickness in a particular tissue?

   (a) Rate of vascular circulation to the tissue
   (b) Amount of nitrogen stored in the tissue
   (c) Rate at which nitrogen can diffuse through the tissue
   (d) Difference between the partial pressure of N_2 in tissue and in the blood
   (e) All the above

41. The Haldane principle is based on what three considerations?

42. Give three contributory factors to decompression illness.

43. If a diver makes a cold and strenuous dive to 70 feet for 60 minutes, he should decompress as though we went to

   (a) 70 feet for 60 minutes
   (b) 70 feet for 70 minutes
   (c) 80 feet for 60 minutes
   (d) 80 feet for 70 minutes

44. When decompressing at a 10-foot stop, one should

   (a) remain still with the head at 10 feet
   (b) remain still with the chest at 10 feet
   (c) exercise with head at 10 feet
   (d) exercise with chest at 10 feet

45. The repetitive dive tables use a minimum surface interval of

   (a) two minutes
   (b) five minutes
   (c) ten minutes
   (d) twenty-five minutes

46. The major result of Professor Haldane's work in 1907 was the development of
    (a) helium-oxygen equipment
    (b) stage decompression
    (c) recompression chambers
    (d) oxygen decompression

47. If you dive to 90 feet, the longest dive without decompression is
    (a) no limit
    (b) 15 minutes
    (c) 25 minutes
    (d) 30 minutes

48. A diver makes a dive to 60 feet with a bottom time of 58 minutes and then does a free ascent in 30 seconds
    (a) He should make a slower ascent on the next dive to compensate.
    (b) He should return to and decompress at 10 feet for at least 30 seconds.
    (c) He should do nothing.
    (d) He should add 10 minutes to his surface interval time.

49. Which of the following factors does not increase a diver's susceptibility to the bends?
    (a) Cold
    (b) High fluid intake
    (c) Heavy exertion
    (d) Tight-fitting wet suit

50. For high altitude diving, decompression time must
    (a) increase
    (b) decrease
    (c) remain the same
    (d) increase by one depth and time interval

51. Residual nitrogen is considered to have completely left the body
    (a) immediately after surfacing
    (b) after one hour
    (c) after twelve hours
    (d) after your surface interval

52. Decompression is used to prevent
    (a) air embolism
    (b) subcutaneous emphysema
    (c) bends
    (d) thoracic squeeze

53. Bottom time is the time from
    (a) arriving on the bottom to leaving the bottom
    (b) beginning of descent to beginning of ascent
    (c) beginning of dive to end of dive
    (d) arriving on bottom to arriving back at surface

54. Recompression by taking the diver down again is not practical because
    (a) the diver would suffer pain at depth
    (b) the pressure required in most cases would require a depth of 100 feet
    (c) sufficient air supply and proper medical attention would not be practical
    (d) the diver giving aid could get the bends

55. A sport diver
    (a) should make very few decompression dives
    (b) is qualified to make decompression dives whenever he needs to
    (c) should never make a dive requiring decompression
    (d) should only make a decompression dive when a recompression chamber is close by

Plan the Following Dives

56. 60 feet   40 minutes D.C. _____ Group _____
2 hour surface interval   Group _____ 60 feet _____
maximum bottom time no decompression.

57. 100 feet   30 minutes D.C. _____ Group _____
6 hours surface interval Group _____ 90 feet 25 minutes D.C. _____
Group _____

58. 30 feet   200 minutes D.C. _____ Group_____
3 hours surface interval   Group _____60 feet _____
maximum bottom time no decompression Group _____

59. 80 feet   60 minutes D.C. _____Group _____
2 hours surface interval Group _____
maximum depth 40 minutes no decompression.

60. 60 feet   120 minutes D.C. _____ Group_____
minimum surface interval   Group _____
60 feet   30 minutes bottom time no decompression

Breathing

61. The correct method of breathing when using scuba is
    (a) fast and shallow
    (b) slow and shallow

    (c) slow and deep

    (d) fast and deep

62. A dangerous breathing pattern that results in no gas exchange and that sometimes occurs under stress is

    (a) overbreathing the regulator

    (b) breathing from the top third of the lungs

    (c) breathing too shallow

    (d) breathing deeply and failing to exhale

63. Excessive hyperventilation prior to free diving could cause

    (a) occurrence of an anoxic condition resulting in loss of consciousness

    (b) blackout due to CO_2 excess

    (c) N_2 narcosis

    (d) convulsions

64. Hyperventilation increases one's ability to stay underwater by

    (a) reducing the oxygen tension in the blood

    (b) washing out the carbon dioxide

    (c) building up an air surplus in the lungs

    (d) increasing the tissue's ability to store oxygen

65. Unintentional hyperventilation can be caused by

    (a) nervous tension

    (b) anoxia

    (c) anxiety

    (d) any of these

Psychological Aspects of Diving

66. The ideal common sense versus physical ability ratio is

    (a) 50:50

    (b) 40:60

    (c) 70:30

    (d) 60:40

67. List four sources of stress to which a diver is subjected.

68. A safe diving philosophy includes

    (a) self-honesty, assumption of responsibilities, defensive buddy concept, and dive planning.

    (b) self-honesty, selectivity, and always diving up to one's own capacity.

    (c) dive planning, diving the plan, and responding to challenge.

    (d) incorporating the defensive buddy system, developing total self-confidence so that the diver can cope with virtually any situation that may occur.

69. Emotional fitness of a diver includes what three factors?
    (a) Awareness, selectivity, and physical competence
    (b) Relaxation, self-honesty, and good watermanship
    (c) Common sense, maturity, and self-discipline
    (d) Motivation, relaxation, and physical fitness
70. When faced with a stressful situation the diver should
    (a) react quickly as any delay may worsen the situation
    (b) worry about the situation before him
    (c) allow the more experienced diver to make all decisions
    (d) stop, think, react
71. Panic is
    (a) a normal flight reaction
    (b) the point when mental consciousness loses control over physical response
    (c) a normal fight reaction
    (d) both b and c
72. Panic may be prevented through self-discipline, anticipation, overtraining, and determination of the exact situation. (True or false)
73. What are the three major responsibilities of a diver?
74. Anxiety
    (a) creates blocks to learning and confident behavior
    (b) is a necessary element in survival
    (c) warns of danger and makes a diver careful in his actions
    (d) all of these
75. The four primary points of a good dive plan are
    (a) determining the air cutoff point, selection of the correct technique, ensuring the dive plan is adhered to strictly, and appointing the most experienced diver as dive master
    (b) ensuring that each diver is properly equipped, training of specialized technique, determining that all air can be used so that none is wasted by returning partially filled tanks to the surface, and planning the dive around the least experienced diver
    (c) determining that each diver understands the group is to surface when the first diver hits reserve or 300 psig, selecting correct technique, establishing a maximum depth and bottom time, and setting the maximum number of divers on the dive
    (d) information gathering, group planning, individual planning, and self-preparation

Different Diving Environments

76. What are three things that cause currents?
77. To escape from a rip current
    (a) swim parallel to the beach
    (b) swim toward the shore
    (c) swim away from the shore
    (d) ride the current out and wait for help
78. List the precautions you would take when making a night dive.
79. List three reasons why cave diving is considered hazardous.
80. There is more likelihood of shark attack
    (a) when visibility is poor
    (b) when carrying speared fish close to the body
    (c) if you are injured or bleeding
    (d) all of these
81. Unexposed offshore reefs can be located by
    (a) the sudden increase in the height of swells
    (b) the change in currents
    (c) white caps
    (d) sea gulls
82. Surf is caused by
    (a) current traveling perpendicular to the beach
    (b) tides reacting from the runoff from the beach
    (c) the lower part of a wave being slowed more than the top, causing an unstable condition
    (d) wind traveling in the same direction as the waves
83. The height of a wave is the
    (a) distance between crest and trough
    (b) distance between two troughs
    (c) distance in elevation from the water surface in the wave trough to the crest of the wave
    (d) distance from bottom of ocean to top of wave
84. Current
    (a) at top is less than at bottom
    (b) at bottom is less than at top
    (c) may be strong at one depth and weak at another
85. Sound travels _____ in water as it does in air.
    (a) approximately 4.5 times as fast
    (b) approximately one-fourth as fast
    (c) about one-half as fast
    (d) about three times as fast

86. The three greatest causes of agony to divers are
    (a) sun, seasickness, and shark
    (b) moray eels, barracuda, and shark
    (c) barnacles, sea urchins, and corals
    (d) bends, air embolism, and drowning

87. The fish that covers itself with sand and may inflict a dangerous wound is the
    (a) moray eel
    (b) sculpin
    (c) manta ray
    (d) stingray

88. Which type of bottom requires the most protective clothing?
    (a) Coral
    (b) Rock
    (c) Gravel
    (d) Sand
    (e) Mud

Equipment

89. If your regulator continually feeds you a fine mist of water, what are the two most likely problems?

90. Draw a diagram of a balanced-piston first-stage regulator, with a downstream second stage.

91. Tanks must be hydrostated every _____ years, and it is recommended that it be visually inspected _____

92. Draw a closed-circuit rebreather.

93. The diver's flag on a float indicates
    (a) divers are down and have the right-of-way over boatmen
    (b) divers are down and boats should keep clear of the area
    (c) the area is reserved for skin and scuba divers
    (d) the float is owned by a skin or scuba diver

94. Which of the following is the most important consideration concerning the administration of artificial respiration?
    (a) Begin as soon as possible
    (b) Use a steady, even pace
    (c) Use deep breaths
    (d) Clear lungs of water

95. The only two major arteries recommended by the American Red Cross for arterial pressure point control of bleeding are
    (a) carotid and brachial
    (b) brachial and femoral

    (c) carotid and femoral

    (d) carotid and jugular

  96. External cardiac massage and mouth-to-mouth resuscitation should be administered in what ratio with one operator? With two operators?

  97. Which of the following conditions would deserve first attention by the first-aider?

    (a) Shock

    (b) Respiratory arrest

    (c) Bleeding

    (d) Cardiac arrest

  98. Give four ways to control bleeding.

  99. What are two symptoms of shock?

  100. The position of a victim that is comatose is on his back with feet elevated approximately 8-12 inches. (True or false)

  101. Mouth-to-mouth resusciation is the resuscitation method favored over all others primarily because the inspired air has a higher percentage of O_2. (True or false)

  102. Vomiting should not be induced in a victim who has ingested gasoline. (True or false)

  103. A compound fracture is one in which the bone is broken in two or more places. (True or false)

  104. In splinting a fracture, it is desirable to immobilize only the broken bone ends. (True or false)

  105. What are three methods used to stop bleeding?

  106. The first aid for a sprain is applications of

    (a) cold, wet towels

    (b) warm, wet towels

    (c) alternate warm and cold towels

    (d) neither wet nor cold towels

  107. The first aid for a strain is applications of

    (a) cold, wet towels

    (b) warm, wet towels

    (c) alternate warm and cold towels

    (d) neither cold or wet towels

  108. For victims of second and third degree burns, you should

    (a) cover the burn with 4 to 6 layers of dry cloth

    (b) cover the burn with 4 to 6 layers of damp cloth

    (c) apply some sort of butter or oil

    (d) apply nothing

Appendix C:

Open Water Evaluation Tests

Watermanship Test A

Skill One: Don mask, fins, and snorkel; surface dive to bottom of pool. Remove mask and snorkel, lay them on bottom. Surface, take three to five breaths maximum. Surface dive, recover and clear mask and snorkel.

```
Mask and snorkel fully clear . . . . . . . . . . . . . . . . . . . . . . . . . . . . . .20 pts
Mask two-thirds clear and snorkel clear  . . . . . . . . . . . . . . . . . . . .16 pts
Mask one-half clear and snorkel clear  . . . . . . . . . . . . . . . . . . . . . .14 pts
Mask clear and snorkel two-thirds clear  . . . . . . . . . . . . . . . . . . . .12 pts
Mask clear and snorkel flooded  . . . . . . . . . . . . . . . . . . . . . . . . . . .8 pts
Mask and snorkel flooded . . . . . . . . . . . . . . . . . . . . . . . . . . . . . . . .0 pts
```

Skill Two: With mask, flippers, and snorkel swim 400 yards

Time (min:sec)	Pts	Time	Pts
0:00-6:00	20	7:11-7:15	13
6:01-6:05	19	7:16-7:20	12.5
6:06-6:10	18	7:21-7:25	12
6:11-6:15	17	7:26-7:30	11.5
6:16-6:20	16.5	7:31-7:35	11
6:21-6:30	16	7:36-7:40	10.5
6:31-6:40	15.5	7:41-7:45	10
6:41-6:50	15	7:46-7:50	9
6:51-7:00	14.5	7:51-7:55	7
7:01-7:05	14	7:56-8:00	5
7:06-7:10	13.5		

Skill Three: Breath control circuit (no surfacing)

(a) Swim 25 yards underwater, breathe on scuba, don mask, flippers, and snorkel
(b) Swim 15 yards; take three breaths from scuba
(c) Swim 10 yards underwater; free ascend; go to surface
    a–c = 20 pts   a–b = 16 pts   a = 12 pts

Skill Four: Ditch and don (deep end of pool)

Time	Pts	Time	Pts
0:00-2:00	20	3:46-4:00	15
2:01-2:20	19	4:01-4:10	14
2:21-2:40	18	4:11-4:20	13
2:41-3:00	17	4:21-4:30	12
3:01-3:15	16.5	4:31-4:40	10
3:16-3:30	16	4:41-4:50	8
3:31-3:45	15.5	4:51-5:00	6

Skill Five: Buddy breathing circuit
(a) Buddy breathe 200 yards
(b) Exchange scuba while buddy breathing
(c) Remove mask, buddy breathe 100 yards
(d) Exchange equipment while buddy breathing, then surface
    a–d = 20 pts   a–c = 16 pts   a–b = 12 pts   a = 8 pts

Watermanship Test B

Skill One: 400-yard swim

Time (min:sec)	Pts	Time	Pts
8:00 or under	20	10:21-10:25	15
8:01-8:20	19.5	10:26-10:30	14
8:21-8:40	19	10:31-10:45	13
8:41-9:00	18.5	10:46-11:00	12
9:01-9:20	18	11:01-11:15	11
9:21-9:40	17.5	11:16-11:30	10
9:41-10:00	17	11:31-11:45	9
10:01-10:10	16.5	11:46-12:00	8
10:11-10:20	16		

Skill Two: Cleaning of mask and snorkel, donning of flippers
Diver places mask, fins, and snorkel on bottom of pool; diver surfaces, takes three breaths, surface dives to bottom of pool, clears mask and snorkel and puts flippers on using only one breath.
Both mask and snorkel fully cleared and flippers on. . . . . .20 pts

Mask *or* snorkel only three-fourths clear and flippers on . . . . . . .15 pts
Mask and snorkel clear but flippers not on . . . . .10 pts

Skill Three: 50-yard underwater swim (swimmer must use three breaths)
Completed swim . . . . .20 pts
Less than three breaths . . . . .15 pts
One extra breath . . . . .10 pts

Skill Four: Ditch and don all equipment except vest

Time	Pts	Time	Pts
0:00-2:00	20	3:46-4:00	15
2:01-2:20	19	4:01-4:10	14
2:21-2:40	18	4:11-4:20	13
2:41-3:00	17	4:21-4:30	12
3:01-3:15	16.5	4:31-4:40	10
3:16-3:30	16	4:41-4:50	8
3:31-3:45	15.5	4:51-5:00	6

Skill Five: Malfunctioning equipment circuit (no surfacing)
   (a) Use regulator with no nonreturn valve (single hose), 25 yards
   (b) Exchange to unit with double-hose regulator, use 25 yards
   (c) Exchange to unit with a regulator that has no holder (tits) on mouthpiece
   (d) Use bare tank for 25 yards
      a–d = 20 pts   a–c = 16 pts   a–b = 10 pts   a = 8 pts

Watermanship Test C

Skill One: With mask, snorkel, and fins swim 880 yards, no hands

Time (min:sec)	Pts	Time	Pts
14:00 or under	20	17:16-17:30	14
14:01-14:30	19.5	17:31-17:45	13.5
14:31-15:00	19	17:46-18:00	13
15:01-15:15	18.5	18:01-18:15	12.5
15:16-15:30	18	18:16-18:30	12
15:31-15:45	17.5	18:31-18:45	11.5
15:46-16:00	17	18:46-19:00	11
16:01-16:15	16.5	19:01-19:15	10.5
16:16-16:30	16	19:16-19:30	10
16:31-16:45	15.5	19:31-19:45	9
16:46-17:00	15	19:46-20:00	8
17:01-17:15	14.5	over 20 min.	0

Skill Two: Normal buddy breathing (circuit 1)
   (a) Buddy breathe 100 yards
   (b) Without surfacing, remove mask and buddy breathe 100 yards
   (c) Remove flippers, buddy breathe 50 yards. Replace flippers, leave mask off
   (d) Surface, but keep face underwater, buddy breathe on snorkel 50 yards
      a–d = 20 pts   a–c = 15 pts   a–b = 10 pts   a = 5 pts

Skill Three: Breath control circuit
   Four scuba units are placed in water with air off—20 yards to first unit, 10 yards to second, 10 more yards to third unit, and 15 yards to fourth unit. Then free ascend over a distance of 10 more yards (Note! For each extra breath taken, 2 points will be deducted. Any time the air is left on, 1 point will be deducted.)
   (a) With mask, snorkel, and flippers, surface dive and swim underwater to first unit. Take two breaths, turn air off and continue likewise through other three units.
   (b) Remove mask and snorkel, repeat same procedure
   (c) Remove all equipment and repeat as an underwater swimmer
      a–c = 20 pts   a–b = 15 pts   a = 8 pts

Skill Four: Diver tow (head of diver being towed must be out of water, towing diver is using scuba) 100 yards

Time	Pts	Time	Pts
2:00-2:10	20	3:01-3:20	10
2:11-2:20	19.5	3:21-3:40	7
2:21-2:30	19	3:41-4:00	5
2:31-2:40	18	4:01-4:20	4
2:41-2:50	16	4:21-4:40	3
2:51-3:00	12	4:41-5:00	2

Skill Five: Lifesaving
   (a) Proper entry into water, swim 25 yards, make rear approach to victim
   (b) Place victim in cross-chest carry, tow him 25 yards
   (c) Switch to tired swimmers, carry for 50 yards
   (d) Then victim gets rescuer in a front headlock; make break, level and tow victim in a control carry 15 yards
      a–d = 20 pts   a–c = 15 pts   a–b = 12 pts   a = 8 pts

Watermanship Test D

Skill One: Scuba swim using snorkel 300 yards

Time (min:sec)	Pts	Time	Pts
9:00 or under	20	10:41-10:50	15.5
9:01-9:15	19.5	10:51-11:00	15
9:16-9:30	19	11:01-11:05	14
9:31-9:45	18.5	11:06-11:10	13
9:46-10:00	18	11:11-11:15	12
10:01-10:10	17.5	11:16-11:20	11
10:11-10:20	17	11:21-11:25	10
10:21-10:30	16.5	11:26-11:30	9
10:31-10:40	16	11:31-12:00	8

Skill Two: Diver and swimmer buddy breathing
   (a) Buddy breathe 50 yards, exchange equipment from diver to swimmer
   (b) Buddy breathe 50 more yards, exchange equipment again, free ascend

   a–b = 20 pts   a = 8 pts

Skill Three: Breath control plus scuba circuit (no surface)
   (a) Swim 25 yards underwater, don scuba, vest, mask, flippers, and snorkel
   (b) With buddy swim to deep end of pool, remove scuba only and free ascend to surface
   (c) Take exactly three breaths, surface dive, don scuba; remove mask and buddy breathe 25 yards

   a–c = 20 pts   a–b = 15 pts   a = 8 pts

Skill Four: Bailout (air off, regulator not in mouth, vest and weight belt are already on).

Time	Pts	Time	Pts
Under 1:30	20	3:01-3:15	12
1:31-1:40	19.5	3:16-3:30	10
1:41-1:50	19	3:31-3:45	7
1:51-2:00	18	3:46-4:00	5
2:01-2:15	17	4:01-4:20	4
2:16-2:30	16	4:21-4:40	3
2:31-2:45	15	4:41-4:40	3
2:46-3:00	14		

Skill Five: Scuba diver lifesaving (subtract 1 point each time victim's head is pushed underwater).
   (a) Rescue unconscious diver from bottom of pool
   (b) Remove mask, administer mouth-to-mouth resuscitation while towing him 25 yards
   (c) With assistance, remove victim from pool, give directions for assistance
   (d) Simulate CPR with one operator (use piece of foam instead of victim's chest)
   a–d = 20 pts   a–c = 15 pts   a–b = 12 pts   a = 8 pts

Watermanship Test E

Skill One: Swim with scuba, mask, flippers using snorkel 400 yards

Time (min:sec)	Pts	Time	Pts
0:00-11:00	20	13:11-13:20	15.5
11:01-11:20	19.5	13:21-13:30	15
11:21-11:40	19	13:31-13:40	14.5
11:41-12:00	18.5	13:41-13:50	14
12:01-12:15	18	13:51-14:00	13
12:16-12:30	17.5	14:01-14:15	12
12:31-12:45	17	14:16-14:30	10
12:46-13:00	16.5	14:31-14:45	8
13:01-13:10	16	14:46-15:00	6

Skill Two: Rescue disabled diver
   (a) Recover diver from bottom of pool (depress disphragm)
   (b) Tow and resuscitate 25 yards
   (c) Remove scuba and get victim out of pool
   (d) Simulate CPR

Time	Pts	Time	Pts
0:00-3:00	20	3:51-4:00	17
3:01-3:20	19.5	4:01-4:20	15
3:21-3:30	19	4:21-4:40	12
3:31-3:40	18.5	4:41-5:00	8
3:41-3:50	18		

Skill Three: Buddy breathe for 30 minutes without surfacing and while constantly swimming. 20 points.

Skill Four: Circuit, no surfacing

(a) Swim 25 yards underwater, don scuba
(b) Scuba swim 25 yards, don mask, snorkel, flippers
(c) Surface, use snorkel, swim 100 yards

Time	Pts	Time	Pts
0:00-3:00	20	4:16-4:20	14
3:01-3:10	19.5	4:21-4:25	13
3:11-3:20	19	4:26-4:30	12
3:21-3:30	18.5	4:31-4:35	11
3:31-3:40	18	4:36-4:40	10
3:41-3:50	17.5	4:41-4:50	9
3:51:4:00	17	4:51-5:00	8
4:01-4:05	16.5	5:01-5:10	6
4:06-4:10	16	5:11-5:20	4
4:11-4:15	15	5:21-5:30	2

Skill Five: Circuit, no surfacing
   (a) Bailout, scuba, 25 yards
   (b) Ditch equipment (except vest), free ascend, take three breaths, surface dive and recover scuba, mask, flippers, and snorkel
   (c) Surface, tread water 5 minutes (regulator and snorkel cannot be used)

Watermanship Test F

Skill One: Octopus buddy breathe 800 yards

Time (min:sec)	Pts	Time	Pts	Time	Pts
0:00-17:00	20	18:01-18:10	17	18:51-1855	13
17:01-17:15	19.5	18:11-18:20	16.5	18:56-19:00	12
17:16-17:30	19	18:21-18:30	16	19:01-19:15	11
17:31-17:40	18.5	18:31-18:39	15.5	19:16-19:30	10
17:41-17:50	18	18:40-18:45	15	19:31-19:45	99
17:51-18:00	17.5	18:46-18:50	14	19:46-20:00	8

Skill Two: Bailout

Time	Pts	Time	Pts	Time	Pts
0:00-1:10	20	1:41-1:45	17.5	2:06-2:10	15
1:11-1:20	19.5	1:46-1:50	17	2:11-2:15	14.5
1:21-1:30	19	1:51-1:55	16.5	2:16-2:30	14
1:31-1:35	18.5	1:56-2:00	16	2:31-2:45	11
1:36-1:40	18	2:01-2:05	15.5	2:46-3:00	8

Skill Three: Diver rescue

    (a) Recover disabled diver from bottom of pool (establish airway, c press diaphragm, and ascend)

    (b) By use of victim's buoyancy compensator adjust for proper buo ancy and administer mouth-to-mouth resuscitation while towi victim

    (c) Remove victim from water (with assistance) and make emergen arrangements, simulate CPR

$$a-c = 20 \text{ pts} \quad a-b = 16 \text{ pts} \quad a = 8 \text{ pts}$$

Skill Four: Breath control

    (a) Swim 25 yards underwater, don scuba, mask, and flippers

    (b) Swim to deep end of pool, ditch scuba, free ascend, take a ma mum of three breaths, surface dive, don scuba

    (c) Ascend to surface and tread water 5 minutes

Time	Pts	Time	Pts	Time	Pts
0:00-8:00	20	9:01-9:10	17.5	9:51-10:00	15
8:01-8:15	19.5	9:11-9:20	17	10:01-10:15	14
8:16-8:30	19	9:21-9:30	16.5	10:16-10:30	13
8:31-8:45	18.5	9:31-9:40	16	10:31-10:45	10
8:46-9:00	18	9:41-9:50	15.5	10:46-11:00	8

Skill Five: Malfunctioning equipment

    (a) Use regulator with no nonreturn valve 25 yards

    (b) Exchange to regulator with no mouthpiece for 25 yards

    (c) Exchange to bare tank for 25 yards

$$a-c = 20 \text{ pts} \quad a-b = 16 \text{ pts} \quad a = 8 \text{ pts}$$

Watermanship Test G

Skill One: Breath control

    (a) With mask and fins, swim 25 yards underwater. Breathe on scul while removing mask

    (b) Swim 25 yards to a second scuba, breathe on scuba while removi flippers

    (c) Swim 25 yards to a third scuba, take three breaths and free asce to surface

$$a-c = 20 \text{ pts} \quad a-b = 16 \text{ pts} \quad a = 8 \text{ pts}$$

Skill Two: Buddy breathing manual 400 yards

Time (min:sec)	Pts	Time	Pts	Time	Pts
0:00-9:00	20	10:11-10:20	17	10:46-10:50	13

9:01-9:20	19	10:21-10:30	16.5	10:51-10:55	12
9:21-9:40	18.5	10:31-10:35	16	10:56-11:00	11
9:41-10:00	18	10:36-10:40	15	11:01-11:30	10
10:01-10:10	17.5	10:41-10:45	14	over 11:30	8

Skill Three: Tow diver 100 yards (both divers in scuba)

Time	Pts	Time	Pts	Time	Pts
0:00-2:00	10	2:41-2:50	17.5	3:46-4:00	15
2:01-2:10	19.5	2:51-3:00	17	4:01-4:15	14
2:11-2:20	19	3:01-3:15	16.5	4:16-4:30	12
2:21-2:30	18.5	3:16-3:30	16	4:31-4:45	10
2:31-2:40	18	3:31-3:45	15.5	4:46-5:00	8

Skill Four: Ditch and don. Time starts when diver enters water and ends upon skill completion.

Time	Pts	Time	Pts	Time	Pts
0:00-1:30	20	1:51-1:55	17.5	2:21-2:30	15.5
1:31-1:40	19	1:56-2:00	17	2:31-2:40	14
1:41-1:45	18.5	2:01-2:10	16.5	2:41-2:50	12
1:46-1:50	18	2:11-2:20	16	2:51-3:00	8

Skill Five

(a) Buddy breathe 100 yards with mask blacked out
(b) Exchange scuba, buddy breathe 100 yards
(c) Re-exchange scuba, remove mask, buddy breathe 100 yards

a—c = 20 pts   a—b = 16 pts   a = 8 pts

Watermanship Test H

Skill One: Control circuit

(a) Swim 25 yards underwater, don tank, mask, and flippers
(b) Swim to deep end of pool, ditch scuba; free ascend; take three breaths surface dive; don scuba
(c) Surface, tread water without use of buoyancy compensator or regulator for 5 minutes

Time (min:sec)	Pts	Time	Pts	Time	Pts
0:00-7:00	20	7:41-7:50	17.5	8:46-9:00	15
7:01-7:10	19.5	7:51-8:00	17	9:01-9:15	14
7:11-7:20	19	8:01-8:15	16.5	9:16-9:30	13
7:21-7:30	18.5	8:16-8:30	16	9:31-9:45	12
7:31-7:40	18	8:31-8:45	15.5	9:46-10:00	8

Skill Two: Buddy breathe 400 yards

Time	Pts	Time	Pts	Time	Pts
0:00-9:00	20	9:46-10:00	17.5	10:41-10:45	14
9:01-9:10	19.5	10:01-10:10	17	10:46-10:50	13
9:11-9:20	19	10:11-10:20	16.5	10:51-10:55	12
9:21-9:30	18.5	10:21-10:30	16	10:56-11:00	10
9:31-9:45	18	10:31-10:40	15	11:01-11:30	8

Skill Three: Scuba swim 800 yards

Time	Pts	Time	Pts	Time	Pts
0:00-16:00	20	17:01-17:10	17.5	18:01-18:20	14
16:01-16:15	19.5	17:11-17:20	17	18:21-18:40	13
16:16-16:30	19	17:21-17:30	16.5	18:41-19:00	12
16:31-16:45	18.5	17:31-17:45	16	19:01-19:30	10
16:46-17:00	18	17:46-18:00	15	19:31-20:00	8

Skill Four: Buddy breathe one mile. 20 points

Skill Five: Buddy breathe 300 yards, blacked-out mask. 20 points

Index

accidents: management of, 95-99; prevention of, 93-95

air: consumption of, 100; planning rules for use of, 89. *See also* cave diving

air embolism: in an accident, 96; defined, 44; related to Boyle's Law, 19; symptoms of, 45; treatment of, 46

altitudes, high, in diving, 66

alveoli, in respiration, 31

Archimede's principle. *See* buoyancy

aseptic bone necrosis, 63

automatic inflator vest, 123

barotrauma, defined, 40

boats: anchoring of, 106; diving from, 107

Boyle's Law: in ascents, 43; breathing resistance, 34; defined, 15-16; in descent, 40; in salvage work, 23

breathing: abnormal patterns of, 97-99; resistance factors in, 34-35. *See also* hyperventilation, dead spaces

BTU (heat measure), 24

bubble formation, 59-61; silent, 59

buddy system, 87-88, 146

buoyancy: computations of the diver, 23; control of, 23, 101; problems of, 85-86

buoyancy compensator, 112, 122

carbon dioxide, 60; limits of, 35-36; related to decompression, 60; stimulus to respiration, 31

carbon monoxide, poisoning by, 36-37

cave diving, 108; air rules for, 112-13; buoyancy in, 114; equipment in, 109; qualifications, 141; swim techniques, 114-15

Charles' Law, defined, 20

circulatory system: defined, 33; heart in, 33; pulmonary, 34; systemic, 34

color, absorption underwater, 25

compass, 123

compressors, 135

current, diving in, 106

Dalton's Law, partial pressures, 21, 22, 51-56

dead spaces, related to breathing resistance, 34

decompression procedures, 69-70; stages of, 65-66

decompression sickness: in accident, 96; and Boyle's Law, 19; bubble formation, 59-62; chamber used in, 136; contributing factors to, 59-62; dehydration in, 60; exercise in, 59, 66; flying, 66; half-times, 65; interrupted, 68-69; prevention of, 65-66; silent bubbles in, 59; stops in, 66; systems of, 62-65; treatment of, 67-68

density: in breathing resistance, 35; of freshwater, 17; of salt water, 17

depth gauge, 16, 121

descending line, 107

diffusion. *See* gases

dive master qualifications, 141

dive plan, 88-89

diver: qualification levels, 139; stages of development, 94. *See also* shallow water diver, intermediate diver, research diver, dive master

dive tables, use of, 121

diving program at RSMAS, 139-46